And I Will Paint the Sky

Women
Speak the Story
of
Their Lives

Carole Trainor, editor

Pottersfield Press
Lawrencetown Beach, Nova Scotia, Canada

Canadian Cataloguing in Publication Data
Main entry under title:
   And I will paint the sky: Women speak the story of their lives

   ISBN 1-895900-39-5

1. Women – Canada – Social conditions. 2. Women – Canada – Biography.
I. Trainor, Carole
FC26.W6W66 2001   305.42'092'271   C2001-900026-X
CT3270.W65 2001

Front cover painting:
   "Facing Kingsmere" by Su Rogers
   photo by Marion Bordier

Pottersfield Press gratefully acknowledges the ongoing support of the Nova Scotia Department of Tourism and Culture, Cultural Affairs Division, as well as The Canada Council for the Arts. We acknowledge the financial support of the Government of Canada through the Book Publishing Industry Development Program for our publishing activities.

Printed in Canada.
Pottersfield Press
83 Leslie Road
East Lawrencetown
Nova Scotia, Canada, B2Z 1P8
To order telephone toll free 1-800-NIMBUS9 (1-800-646-2879)

THE CANADA COUNCIL FOR THE ARTS SINCE 1957 | LE CONSEIL DES ARTS DU CANADA DEPUIS 1957

NOVASCOTIA Tourism and Culture

Canada

For my mother, M.B. Walker

Je me souviens de toi, ma mére.

Je n'ai pas oubliée. Je n'oublierai jamais! . . .

Toi, la plus grande des artiste dans ton amour pour moi. . . .

La plus grande des artiste!

(I remember you, my mother.

I do not forget. I will never forget! . .

Artist of all artists in your love for me . . .

artist of all artists! . . .)

With thanks to Cheryl Downton
for keeping her integrity
and
for loving truth.

Contents

Foreword   9

Dr. Heather Zitner   15

Diann Graham   22

Rea Shaw   33

Anne-Marie Woods   37

Linda Harpell   55

Anne S. Derrick   60

Lorri Neilsen   65

Wanda Thomas Bernard   78

Erie Maestro   96

Terry March   106

Cheryl Downton   117

Maureen MacDonald   123

Julie Godwin   133

Candace Bernard   144

Leah M.F. Caitlin   155

Patti Doyle-Bedwell   162

Foreword

In October of 1999, I proposed a number of courses to the Nova Scotia Community College on Bell Road, Halifax. One of the courses was entitled "Women of Halifax." I'm not sure exactly how the idea came about, but it was, undoubtedly, born of my frustration with the ways images of young female people continue to be offered up as commercial prey for the consumption of mainstream culture. Much to my surprise and excitement, the college accepted the idea and within months the Women of Halifax course was listed in the winter term calendar of the Nova Scotia Community College.

Thanks to a suggestion given me by Dr. Wanda Thomas Bernard of the Maritime School of Social Work, I contacted a local publisher, Lesley Choyce, and told him of my plan to gather brief autobiographies from local women as a way of educating the public about women's courage and heroism. Mr. Choyce was receptive to the idea and within no time at all, the idea, and the project itself, began receiving some local media attention.

Throughout the process of gathering these relatively personal stories, interacting with each of the women on a somewhat intimate basis, I realized I had created for myself a life-altering experience. I think that I am in many ways because of this project less naïve now, less idealistic about humankind in general. I realize that not every woman cares about the welfare of other women. I don't know that I really *knew* this before embarking on this project. I saw my *passion* for that which concerns women as a natural extension of my humanity, and therefore a generic kind of trait. I see now that this is more specific to me as a person. I keep in mind as I say this, of course, the many influences that have shaped me. I keep in mind the tremendous impact Lesbian scholarship has had on my intellectual processes, and on my inside redefinition of "self." I have, over the years, become so affected and so impassioned by the writing and scholarship of lesbian women that I am unable to remember a time when lesbian thought wasn't completely woven through the fabric of my entire mind/body. This factor combined with other strong influences in my life, such as the love and friendship of one extraordinary woman, Cheryl Downton, has afforded me a way to go beyond the self-denying, self-negating script of traditional female heterosexuality.

I learned through the glorious feedback of some of the women involved in this project that true female comradery is alive and well. I also learned that some of the toughest among us are perhaps the most tender, the most idealistic. I am charmed by Maureen MacDonald's story of wanting to "take in" every stray cat that crossed her path as a child. I am charmed to think that Anne Derrick held to her youthful dream of bringing justice to the world. All of these women have surprised and intrigued me with their stories. All of these women have helped to create this raw, unique, most intimate profile with their honesty and personal integrity. I will always be grateful for the eager and passionate participation of the women involved.

It always amazes me how quickly we as human beings find ways to separate ourselves from each other, how quickly we find ways to draw lines between that which we feel defines *us* and that which we feel defines the *other*. I like to think that for a few quick moments the tide was able to wash over the lines we as women have drawn in the sand, in order that this collective expression of stories be told. How hard it becomes now to get back behind the lines that separate me from them, as I attempt to bring closure to this extraordinary experience. It has been a privilege to have been allowed to pass back and forth between camps, between women's worlds, for even a very brief period of time.

As a person, I am made prouder for this project. As a woman, I am made surer. I am at once able to testify that I have suffered the slings and arrows every lover must suffer as she embarks upon the dangerous territory of that which she loves with great passion. I have struggled to maintain the integrity of this collection of stories, and I have refused to lighten it with any artificial "gleeful" sentiment. As I see it, my task as editor is to convey to you, the reader, truthful, uncompromised representations. I feel sure that this has been accomplished.

This book would not be able to lay claim to its artful nature were it not for the suffering of those of us who believe in the power of women's uncompromised story telling — for those of us burning with the honest need to "tell" our lives the way we live them. I have passed through many emotions as I entered the worlds of each of these women. Some of the stories I embraced with great enthusiasm. I was proud to find pieces of me there. Other stories frightened, embarrassed, and disturbed me. I am unable, however, to see how it can be any other way, as long as our subjective experiences as women remain in the dark corners of mainstream thought. I am unable to see how we as women can move closer to self-love or self-acceptance without going beyond our own psychological comfort zones. Clearly, this project took me beyond the boundaries of my own psychological safety. Clearly, this project unsettled and disrupted my intellectual calm. I am not sorry for this, in spite of the fact that I must live with the painful pieces, pieces that continue to unsettle and disrupt my notions of who it is I think am inside this female skin.

I am glad to be able to put a close to the work involved in pulling aspects of this book together, but I am, of course, saddened to have to say goodbye. I went very quickly from being a somewhat timid educator offering a very modest course, to someone tossing her own ideas about in the office of a book publisher! I have been privileged indeed. Watching a single idea come out of an abstract web of thoughts, watching it land onto the keypad, feeling it travel through the telephone cord only to land on the desk of publisher Lesley Choyce, who says "Yes, why not you?" is an indescribable feeling. I will always be grateful to Lesley Choyce for deeming the subject matter of this book worthy enough to publish. I will always be grateful to him for his decision to move forward on this kind of project, at this time.

I myself was born on Prince Edward Island, a place that undoubtedly helped to shape me by intellectually frustrating me to no end. Where I come from, the city of Charlottetown was (perhaps still is) a "father-knows-best" town. I have strong Irish Catholic roots, and so it stands to "reason" then that it wasn't so long ago I was on my knees praying for the poor Protestants who, like the well-intended, church-going women of the day, never seemed to make it out of purgatory.

My mother, having come from a somewhat privileged life in Prince Edward Island — her father being the editor of our local newspapers — met and married my impoverished father against the wishes of one or both of her parents. My mother, willful and determined in spite of it, married the man who would be my father mainly (she told me later) because she'd been charmed by the way he (unlike the privileged boys) "cursed" and "spit." I don't suppose that this knowledge was anything my mother supposed I'd write on paper someday, but I believe that life has its own way of pulling us behind the stories that demand to be told.

My father was undoubtedly a James Dean kind of character for my mother's enlivened imagination, and although he was a brilliant and charismatic performer, a character of impeccable timing, (they'd met in amateur theatre) it was my mother who awed me with the genius and pizzazz of her every cryptic intellectual move.

I have been a social activist, family mediator and educator for some years now. I am a rigorous and passionate thinker who considers the formulation of new thought my greatest challenge, my greatest obligation, and my greatest art.

I have always been troubled by the ways in which brilliant gutsy women have been portrayed throughout the media, and how these images get reinforced throughout our mainstream educative practices. I have often wished that someone would compile stories of local women's lives, so that we, the public at large, could see beyond the anemic images of *femininity* as manufactured by the media. The following stories then are a consequence of this wish realized. A robust thanks to Dr. Wanda Thomas Bernard for her ingenious suggestion; an equally robust thanks to Dr. Lorri Nielsen for her brilliantly poetic phrase: "And I Will Paint the Sky."

Carole E. Trainor

Dr. Heather Zitner, MD

just got back! It's a very long way from there to here. You see, I just spent a week in Poland visiting five labour/death camps and then a week in Israel celebrating the renewal of Jewish life there. This trip occurs every other year when 7,000 teens from all over the world make such a pilgrimage. I was the doctor for 150 of these kids; there were three bus loads of teens and chaperones. How, you may ask, does it happen that a girl from a British Crown Colony makes such a trip? Well, I'll tell you.

I was born when Newfoundland wasn't even part of Canada — most of us are immigrant one way or another. My mother was a "war bride" (they met in Scotland) but didn't marry until after World War II and so I was born to an "elderly primipara" and there were no more kids. My mother helped my father in his business — he was a jeweler. There was no question of partnership — it was his business and she "helped" and also ran the household. Being in retail was all consuming for them and they made a good living, but there was not the security of a biweekly pay cheque and a pension at the end of many years of service.

My mother always emphasized studies as the road to an easier and more secure life and so I was studious. My father would have preferred a more "well-rounded" child; he had been very athletic and identified a lack of that in me; but in all fairness, in the '50s competitive sports were not done by young ladies. It is a small wonder that I was started in a private British type school at age four and wore a tie and tunic until I graduated at age sixteen. We had oral exams in mental arithmetic, French, and current events. I always got good marks and did as I was told; I think the common expression my kids would now use is that I was a "nerd." This was an all girls school and I never even met a boy until the age of fourteen, (no brothers, no male cousins). It would make a great story to say I then went wild with reckless abandon, but that would not be true, so I won't embellish this. I had lots of good girl friends and then dated only one boy in high school — he is now a geophysicist. No skin heads, no rock stars, no "bad boys."

When I was very young, I wanted to be a flight-attendant — we traveled a bit to see my mother's family in Britain, to Florida, etc, but somewhere before I was twelve I decided to be a doctor. No one else in the family had ever done anything in the health professions (my father went to what now is Ryerson in Toronto). I don't remember it as a divine revelation, just a quiet growing conviction that that was what I wanted. I was fascinated with the differences in human bodies as I saw them and wanted to know how they worked, why the differences — and I had the commonly expressed desire to help people. Also, given my upbringing, I felt I wanted a secure profession — no Mom and Pop business for me. Please note the irony in this as you will read later.

My hero as a kid was Marie Curie — imagine a woman scientist. I only knew women as housewives and mothers. No women in my environment worked outside the home in a responsible job of her own. I never knew either of my grandmothers — they were stay-at-home moms. They both died before I was born and both my aunts were career wives and mothers, unlike my uncle who was a lawyer. My mother always resented that formal education was for the brother. So you see, I had no personal role models of the independent professional woman but my mother imbued in me the notion that what was to her unattainable was, by far, preferable.

In school one could choose home economics or Latin — I can still chant *amo, amas, amat, amamous, amatis, amant* — lot of good that did me. In high school I made another dumb move — I chose "academics" not "commercial," meaning I chose not to learn to type — I was going to grow up to *employ* a secretary, not be one. This decision I have regretted for the rest of my life, stupid, stupid, stupid! My mother used to say "knowledge is easily carried about," so I now see most things that happen to me, whether I like them or not, as opportunities to learn and I try to be grateful for the lessons.

When it came time to choose a university, I was very nervous because I would be barely sixteen at the time of entry and the rule was you had to be seventeen; I was genuinely surprised when I was accepted with a scholarship. It never occurred to me to go out of town — all my friends were going to Memorial University in Newfoundland and living at home, but the choice of course was another matter.

Somewhere along the high school years I had lost the expectation I could do medicine and I chose psychology as a "helping" profession and I'm not sorry I did; it was a great undergraduate program. In those days it was a small department with no graduate school and I got to know the professors quite well and got an early introduction to research methodology and practice. I really thrived in that environment. After third year, I applied to be an exchange student in the labs of some Dalhousie psychology professors and something happened that changed the course of my life. I applied for two jobs and accepted the first offer. A day or two later, the second, more preferable job came through. I had already accepted the other one and was squirming for a few days, but my father said to do the honorable thing and stay with my original commitment. I did and came to Dalhousie University and soon met my husband and, as they say, the rest is history.

17

I went on to receive a bachelor and masters degree in psychology and my husband and I played leap-frog for many years — he worked, I went to school, I worked and he went to school. Watching the women in his medical class I began to get that old time feeling — if they can do it, I'm just as smart and can work just as hard, then why can't I? So with the encouragement of my husband I did apply and, after some up-grading, was accepted.

In those days, people got into medical school with only two years of undergraduate training, but I had two degrees and had worked at the Nova Scotia Hospital for two years. So instead of being one of the youngest undergrads, I was one of the older medical students. Our class was only 15 percent women, and I think being already married had great advantages — there was just no sexual tension between me and male classmates — I was just "one of the guys." I wasn't out to meet people and hang out at the frat house. I went to school, came home, did my homework and housework, and the four or five couples in school socialized a bit. I guess I was back to being a nerd. But I was very happy — we had an apartment and even a car, ate well and took simple vacations home. Even the debt load wasn't too bad — only three years of both of us being in school and we considered inviting the banker to the graduation along with the parents!

I don't remember many women lecturers in school; one in microanatomy but in the clinical years it was different. There were several practicing physicians who were women but most were single or had no children. That wasn't a life I wanted. There were again few role models but there was one for whom I had and still have enormous respect. She was very clever, organized and ran her "team" in a soft, quiet manner, but there was no mistake what was expected of you and not meeting those expectations was not even to be considered. She was married with three kids, dressed in a stylish manner and was even very pretty. Now that was who I wanted to be like. You know, I never told her how important she was in my life — but it's never too late; maybe next time I consult her I'll actually say something after the business is over.

There are few medicine superwoman like her; my generation was a "swing" one — most of us felt we had to prove ourselves just as capable and hard working as the men *and* run a tight ship at home. Many modern female physicians know most of us can't do that for long and they unabashedly don't try — they work less hours at the office and more at home in whatever combination works for them and their partners. Bravo!

My first child was born when I was a fourth year clinical clerk — August 1974. I thought the nausea was gall bladder disease for several months. She came a week early when I was on psychiatry rotation and then I took a month annual vacation and went back to work one week late on my pediatric rotation — I had convinced the professor that I was doing on the job training. I would like to tell you that I worked day and night and still nursed her or fed her frozen breast milk, but the truth is after I got back to work mother nature didn't cooperate and Messers Meade and Johnson fed her — and she's the tallest of my kids.

Two more babies followed every three and a half years and I took more time off with the birth of each child. Actually the mid '70s to the mid '90s are a blur to me — I have home movies to prove I was there, but between establishing a career and a family I was very busy. Don't ask me about world events of those two decades — I didn't surface until about 1993.

In 1977, I suffered my first tragic loss. My mother died suddenly while on vacation in Florida. Although I had been away from home for ten years and was twenty-eight years old, I still grieved terribly. My oldest child was only eighteen months old. It pains me that my mother never met my two other children and their births were a bit less joyous for me because I couldn't share it with her. We have a religious service to remember the dead each September, and sometimes, over twenty years later, I still cry for my lost mother. My children never knew her and I never got the benefit of her wisdom on such topics as menopause, cross-cultural marriage, and even the old family history and traditions. I always thought there would be plenty of time for that later, but later never came.

In the '90s, one of my children became seriously ill, and I think it was more difficult for us than for the average parents because we needed to be there for her and to check out the medical care offered. In retrospect, we could have just trusted the local care, which was excellent, but I guess it was an attempt to feel in control of the most unimaginable horror of our lives. She survived, her sisters survived, and we survived but it took an enormous toll.

One of the most enjoyable parts of my practice has been maternity care — I'm a connoisseur of the pregnant belly and much to my daughters' chagrin I'm still a baby freak. I have in my career delivered several thousand babies and the bloom never goes off the rose. It is an indescribable thrill to watch a mother first hear her child's heart beat in utero and then to hear that infant's first cry in the world outside. I never tire of it; that thrill is utterly addictive. You've got to be crazy to relish getting out of your warm bed at 2 a.m., scraping the ice off your car and racing to the hospital with your heart in your throat — will everything be okay for both patients, mother and child? I did it for twenty-five years and only gave up when it became too much for me physically. I know very clearly all the huge number of things that can go wrong (sometimes they tragically do) and it never ceases to amaze me that God makes it right most of the time.

Remember I said no Mom and Pop business for me? Well, my husband and I practiced together for twenty-five years; we spelled each other off at the office and at home and have three magnificent daughters to show for it, and I hope a number of lives on whom there has been a positive influence. The more things change the more they stay the same.

I have been, I think, a very average family doctor, but I have also enjoyed doing some fairly atypical things too. I worked for three years in an inner city health care centre that looked after aboriginal and immigrant patients from Southeast Asia, Central America and East Africa. It was a huge challenge to deliver modern Western medicine in a culturally sensitive fashion. I've also treated Kosovo refugees and have looked at the practice of medicine in the Middle East. Did you know some traditional Bedouin women manage an obstructed labour by hanging by the elbows from the branches of the acacia tree? I also spent some time working at a medical supply base as a volunteer in the Israeli army and I enrolled in a total immersion live-in Hebrew language school for a month.

My kids have cross-cultural interests too; all went to French Immersion School from grade primary and all have traveled extensively — one's now in Sweden and another in Australia and the youngest became Bat Mitzvah in Israel. I think they have all learned no cultural group has cornered the market on distinction or depravity, but we are all very proud to be Canadian.

I'm now going to sound like a Jewish Mother but that's fitting. Food expresses cultural differences and similarities, and cooking and eating together are great builders of community and "warm fuzzy" feelings. I have some Arab and Jewish Israeli friends whose salad is identical, and my friend's mother's (from Romania) strudel is identical to my late mother-in-law's (from Poland). When I worked at the clinic downtown, we had pot luck frequently — it's impossible to have great conflicts when you're sharing each other's traditional foods. I've learned a lot from my friends and their mothers as we cook; I find the older I get and with the exit of my children, the more I value the time we spend together and the personal handing down of traditions in the kitchen and in my life. The things we discuss as we dry dishes and chop vegetables — Will the peace hold across the "Good Fence" in Lebanon/Israel? What will the city be like at the time of the Tall Ships? Which mint is better for tea?

When I was young I thought I was the director of my life and was making all the choices. Now I see there is a pattern, that there are very few coincidences, that things happen for a reason, that I'm a very small cog in a very big wheel. How else can you explain it that a little girl from St. John's is just back from Poland and the stones representing the communities of Lodz and Brok at Treblinka?

21

Diann Graham

Being true to my political beliefs

S ince I moved to Halifax in 1979, the years have gone by in a whirlwind of activity and accomplishment. Sitting back and writing about what I have done over the past twenty years, I am aware of feeling smug, but I realize that my smugness springs from the sense of pride I have in my association with the women with whom I have worked. In typical women's fashion, I look to my relationships and my sense of connectedness with women to explain my accomplishments.

People have asked me why I do the work I do and the short answer is, "I enjoy it." I believe that it is important for all women to engage in political and social action to promote the equality of women. We can do this in our personal and our public lives. When I work for change for myself and for others, I feel energized and empowered. As I work for and with other women, my positive regard for them increases.

As I see myself reflected in their strength and accomplishment, I develop a better self-image and self-esteem.

In a misogynist society, one of the primary issues that all women confront is self-hatred, whether that is reflected in our own negative body image or dislike for other women. The nature of our connectedness with women friends, family members and other social supports is a good indicator of how a woman views herself. Want to feel better about yourself? Then work to develop a better society for all women. I have always held this to be a simple, but important, guideline for addressing complex social problems.

I was born in 1951 and grew up in Nackawic, a small rural community in New Brunswick whose livelihood was rooted in the forestry industry. I was the second of five children born to parents of United Empire Loyalist ancestry. I was brought up in the Baptist religion with a strong Protestant work ethic. I received a Bachelor of Arts degree from Acadia University in 1973 and a Bachelor of Education degree (1980) and a Master of Education degree (1987) from Dalhousie University.

My high school, university and growing-into-adulthood experiences coincided with the beginning of the modern women's movement — 1965–75 was a time of great social/political upheaval. The United Nations declared 1975 as International Women's Year. It was a time which brought about changes in mindset and policy which have affected every aspect of our present society.

There are some moments of discovery in our lives that become crystallized forever in our minds. Moments when you see a direction you should follow. While in high school, I remember seeing on the front page of a local newspaper a picture of a women's liberation march in some big American city where the women were "burning their bras." This taught me a few lessons. If you want to get media coverage, you have to do something spectacular. If you want to get a message out, like "women are oppressed as sexual objects by sexism," you can best illustrate this by taking symbolic action. Those who grasp the symbolism will develop an awareness and become educated. From these spotlight images, a defining moment evolves that helps to form part of a broader social consensus or culture of knowledge. So the image of the feminist bra-burners is part of my heritage and a proud part of that.

I value social action. I believe that disadvantaged people must build an infrastructure that promotes justice. I have not spent a lot of time attacking those who, by word or deed, maintain the oppressive systems that stereotype women. I want to be part of the development of new social orders that empower women and enrich society. I would sooner be proactive and create a new way of being than be always reacting to the insults and indignities of sexism. Others can take up that work; my piece will be building, creating and envisioning.

Drawing from these values, I have put my energies into the creation of five institutions that affirm and support the women of Halifax. In my work, I have tried to remain true to my political beliefs.

Women's Employment Outreach

On March 24, 1980, its first day of operation, I started to work for Women's Employment Outreach (WEO) where I continue to work today. WEO is a grass roots feminist, community-based agency providing employment-related services to women. It began as an initiative of the YMCA which had applied for federal funding from Human Resources Development Canada (formerly CEIC) to provide employment counselling for women. It was established to work towards the economic, social and political equality of women.

Alexa MacDonough, the current leader of the federal New Democratic Party and MP for Halifax, was a volunteer at the Y and wrote the original funding proposal for WEO. Alexa's interests and community activities, even at that time, showed that she had the heart and drive to be where she is today. Alexa remains a friend and supporter of WEO; on March 24, 2000, she delivered the keynote address at WEO's twentieth birthday party.

WEO's feminist principles have guided its organization. We keep in the forefront of all our programs and services the best interests of our clients as women. We function as a collective; power and authority are shared by staff and the volunteer group of women who form WEO's Support Committee. Decisions are reached by consensus. Everyone's voice is heard. Problems are dealt with openly and honestly. Genuine respect and mutual trust is fundamental to everything done by the staff and Support Committee. WEO's empowering process leads to a very productive and pleasant work environment. The staff believes that how we treat each other will be reflected in the way we treat our clients, so we had better get it right! One of the great joys of my life has been seeing this organizational method actually work.

WEO's "women's only" policy is a crucial part of the energy of the agency. Women's economic and political disadvantages grow out of a sexist, misogynist society, dominated by patriarchal institutions. The psyche of society and everything in it is designed for men. Because men are the norm, they have access to all employment counselling services that have been established in consideration of their needs. For that reason, WEO felt it was important to create a small corner or a space in the city that would specifically be for women's benefit.

Since its birth twenty years ago, WEO has had a total of thirteen staff members and sixty-one volunteers in its Support Committee. It has maintained a staff complement of three full-time counsellors, with the addition of an office manager in 1999. In 1992, after completion of a self-review, WEO recognized the importance of hiring an employment counsellor of African-Canadian heritage to address the double barrier to employment which Black women face. Since that time, WEO has had a Black counsellor on staff, which has created a new dynamic in our workplace and allowed us to participate in the community coalitions working to end racism. The perspectives and priorities that the Black counsellors have brought to decision-making and consciousness-raising have educated and enriched my life.

Her-oes

Two of my heroes are my past co-workers, Linda Roberts, with whom I worked from 1980-89, and Jane Andres, from 1984-95. My third hero is a political collective which fought for the rights of women to have a space to be heard.

Linda Roberts and I were the first employees hired at WEO. When WEO first opened, there was funding for only one and a half staff. Linda was the "one" and I was the "half." The funder, CEIC, did not increase the staff allotment as we had requested for the 1981 contract. I went to the Support Committee and asked them to make two equal positions of three-quarter time each. Linda was against this since it would mean a decrease in her salary. After the Support Committee weighed both of our submissions, they decided to support my request. Linda is my hero because she accepted the decision of the collective and continued to be very supportive and positive to me as a co-worker. The foundation of much of WEO's strength and integrity lies in the kind of vision and ethics Linda brought to the work.

Jane Andres weighed all information before making a major decision, thinking about it carefully and then telling us her gut reaction. Jane's "gut feeling" was a guiding light in many decisions. As a co-worker she never faltered from her beliefs and could make tough calls. For example, in 1993 Human Resources Development Canada decided that women were "no longer a priority" and that WEO should become a generic service, also seeing men. If we did not make this change, HRDC threatened to cut our funding.

Faced with the choice of "seeing men or perhaps losing our jobs," Jane said very clearly that principles are more important than pay cheques and that WEO could not let our clients and women of our community down: "We must stand firm against the erosion of services for women." From WEO's perspective, to drastically alter or slash services to women in order to provide services to men was unacceptable and fundamentally affronted our basic feminist principles. After many meetings and considerable lobbying, HRDC bowed to our position and continued WEO's funding to provide services as in the past. Although the threat of cutbacks and closure have continued to hang over us, we are reminded at these times of the principled positions taken by strong women, like Jane.

The Pandora collective is another of my heroes. About ten years after International Women's Year, a backlash took place against women's programs by men who claimed these discriminated against them. One of the most highly publicized cases of such a backlash took place in Halifax and involved Pandora Publishing, a monthly newspaper devoted to stories and news coverage "by, for and about women." In 1992 a Human Rights complaint was laid by a man who claimed discrimination because *Pandora* would not publish his letter to the editor. The inquiry ruled that *Pandora* was protected under the Human Rights Charter that allowed designated groups, like women, who are characterized by persistent conditions reflecting disadvantage, to undertake prescribed programs directed at eliminating inequities.

Unfortunately, soon after the victory *Pandora* ceased operations as a volunteer collective. Its energy and money had been depleted. However, the Pandora Publishing collective empowered women, and affirmed the importance of women having a place to voice their concerns. *Pandora*'s huge victory which forged the right to "women only" programs helped to educate Halifax about the need for such programs to overcome historic systematic discrimination. WEO, whose programs similarly promote equity, greatly benefitted from *Pandora*'s hard-fought victory.

Building on dreams

In December 1999, *The Coast* newspaper published a list of "7 Champions of Women." It was with great pride that I saw Women's Employment Outreach on that list. It was with joy and satisfaction that I also saw Stepping Stone and the Elizabeth Fry Society listed. I have been involved in the conceptualizing and founding of these and other groups that have gone on to prosper. Services and support are in place because of the efforts I made and because of dreams I believed in.

In 1980, I was one of a small group of women who formed the Halifax Women's Housing Cooperative (HWHC), the first women's co-op in Canada. The initiative grew out of the Canada Mortgage and Housing Corporation's (CMHC) Co-op Program which provided opportunities for low income people to, as a group, buy or build urban homes. At the time, low income women confronted a situation of less than 1 percent vacancy rate in rental apartments; an 18 percent mortgage rate made it impossible for women to buy their own homes.

Unable to solve their housing problems individually, six women decided to form a housing co-op that would provide homes for up to twenty members and their children. Using a combination of their own incomes and grants from CMHC, these women, mostly in their twenties, mortgaged and renovated, managed and maintained properties in Halifax which today are valued at over half a million dollars.

None of the original members still live in the HWHC. We have gone on in our careers, moved and/or purchased our own homes. However, it gives me great satisfaction to drive by the HWHC houses and think about how the present day co-op members are carrying on the work that I helped to initiate. I think about the hours of "sweat equity" I did in repairing, doing carpentry, tearing down, and rebuilding the houses. I think with joy about the optimism of the young women who took possession of the run-down properties in 1981-82 and built life back into them. The audacity we had to think that we could do what we did as a group of six women! It is said that "To know women's personal lives is to know the politics of their situation." The Halifax Women's Housing Cooperative is one tangible example of how the "personal is political."

In 1981-83, I was part of a group of women that organized the first "women only" Take Back the Night March. This march has become a yearly event that builds solidarity among women seeking an end to violence against women. Women will never be equal in a society that promotes male violence against them as a form of domination and social control. The march illustrates how women should be able to walk safely on the streets without male protection or permission. It is an exhilarating feeling to be out at night en mass with women, feeling strong and safe. Every woman should take part in one Take Back the Night March.

Along with lawyer Anne Derrick, I co-founded the Women's Alliance in Support of Prostitutes (WASP), an ad hoc group of concerned women which existed from 1983-85. Through my work at WEO, I met a client who was a young drug-addicted prostitute. Although she wanted to leave street life, she was unable to break free of the barriers of poverty, addiction and lifestyle. I decided to become involved in helping to provide support for her and other poor, socially disadvantaged women like her.

Through WASP we provided a drop-in centre for street prostitutes one night a week (located in WEO's office). At night we did street strolls in the areas frequented by prostitutes. We talked to women, gave them information on legal, health and safety issues and generally tried to be supportive, without interfering in them making their own decisions. I spent many a cold winter night trooping down Hollis Street on the stroll. Eventually, WASP's volunteers tired and the organization disbanded. But, because of its work in showing the great need, the government subsequently funded Stepping Stone to provide a direct service to prostitutes.

Shortly after I met that first young prostitute at WEO, she was murdered by a "bad date" — stabbed a number of times and left to bleed to death on a snowy night in the south end of Halifax. While I felt strengthened by my work with WASP, as I write this story my heart still fills with sadness recalling this young woman's death. A civilized society like ours must be judged by how we treat the most disadvantaged and the most downtrodden of our citizens. If we walk along a shoreline dominated by prosperity and beauty, we have to remember to turn over a few rocks to see who inhabits the underside. Both parts make up our city- and mindscape.

As an employment counsellor at WEO, part of my job was to provide employment counselling to women in the Halifax Correctional Centre. It became quickly obvious that my advocating for the women could result in me being denied access to the Correctional Centre. I wanted to become part of a lobby group which could advocate on behalf of women in conflict with the law. I joined with Mary-Liz Greene, a social worker, and others in a small group with similar concerns to form the Halifax Elizabeth Fry group. In 1983, I attended the Canadian Association of Elizabeth Fry Societies (CAEFS) representing the newly formed Halifax group, speaking to the needs of Halifax's women in conflict with the law and requesting application into the national Society. Our membership was approved.

On its tenth anniversary, the Elizabeth Fry Society honoured its founding foremothers. On my office wall, I proudly display the certificate of appreciation I was presented at that time. I remember those early days of the Elizabeth Fry Society with fondness.

I feel that we, in these fledgling organizations, were able to persevere because of our feminist commitment. Whether it was because of our concerns for women we met in prison or street prostitutes, all were strong women who faced very complex barriers. In 1985 I wrote an article for *Pandora* entitled "Many in Prison No Different Than You or Me," in which I talked about how, despite our different circumstances, women have an amazing amount in common. This was one of the fundamental discoveries made by women in the 1960s in "consciousness raising" groups and it still remains true.

In 1983, a royal commission headed by Judge Rosa Abella crisscrossed Canada holding a series of hearings regarding the Status of Women. At that time I wrote and co-presented a statement on behalf of WEO. Seventeen years later, I see that the inequalities we identified then are the same we struggle to overcome today. In 1979, the federal government made women a "priority" and directed funding into programs that would eradicate discrimination and inequality. By 1994, the government no longer considered women a priority for funding or programs. And yet, from the International Women's Year in 1975, through the Royal Commission Report, and into the next millennium, it's clear that the goal of true gender equality is still to be achieved.

Sharing our stories

Faced with a choice of taking any action or doing nothing, I think that I would always choose action. I believe that to outwit patriarchal oppression, the best thing any woman can do is to be happy. If you think of all of the forces of sexism and discrimination that oppress and depress women, finding a space to be happy is a revolutionary act for women.

I have a happy life. As I grow older, I try to spend even more time enjoying myself and the simple pleasures of life. I live with my partner and a small white dog in our home in central Dartmouth. I love to sit on my garden swing under the big maple tree. I am an avid gardener and take great pride in the workings of my compost box, the height of my dahlias, and the colour of my phlox. My partner, my dog and I can be found most weekends walking in the park or along a beach. When I cozy up on the sofa to read a good book (biographies are my favourite), my dog is sound asleep in her bed beside the wood stove. I am also an amateur photographer; over the years I have compiled a photo history of the people, places and events in the Halifax women's community over the past two decades. A little snap camera is my art form.

I have a large circle of women friends whom I look to for love and support. Many enjoyable hours are spent in visiting, activities, phone calls, correspondence and e-mails. I love to cook and prepare large festive meals and listen to the laughter and conversation of my guests. I have perfected my mother's Maritime baked beans recipe and it is counted on as a staple at our frequent pot luck suppers. I also know how to make a to-die-for pineapple upside-down cake.

I have written about some of the work I have done. Because this is a brief autobiography, I have not talked about my activities with the International Women's Day Committee, the Steering Committee of the Lesbian Conference, the Women in Trades Organization, the Advisory Committee to Matrix Women's Program (for women with addictions), the Lesbian Outdoor Club, or the Collins House Emergency Shelter for

Women. There are many more stories I could tell, but I feel it is time for another woman to step forward to tell of her life.

It has been an honour to have been given this opportunity to celebrate my experiences. Perhaps I will stop now and ask each woman who has just read my story to reflect on her own life story. Inside each woman's heart is the story of her own struggles, successes, failures and joys. Share your story with another woman. There is power in your words.

Rea Shaw

counsellor, Bryony House

I was born in Northern Ireland and lived there until 1987 when my family and I came to live in Dartmouth. My husband came to work at the Bedford Institute of Oceanography. Our children were nine and seven at the time. My husband's job was supposed to be for one year so it was not such a big wrench for us to leave Northern Ireland. Not long after we arrived the job was extended for two years and then permanently. So here we all are, still here, after thirteen years!

Prior to coming to Dartmouth I had been employed by Coleraine Women's Aid. I had been part of the original support group that started a refuge for battered women and their children in 1978. Looking back we were very young and very inexperienced but our energy and total commitment to what we were doing compensated for any lack of experience, and we opened the refuge and it is still running. Last year they moved into an incredible purpose-built complex that looks rather like Southfork. A far cry from the big barrack-like former hotel that we started in. I keep in touch with all my friends there and get together with them whenever I am home. In some ways I find it sad that twenty odd years on we still need refuges. At the time we were starting in the movement we thought that refuges would be a temporary thing, needed only for a year or two until attention was drawn to the plight of violence against women, until the law was changed, and women and children would not be driven from their homes by violence.

When I came to Halifax I had decided that I wanted to move away from shelter work and to that end I got a job in the federal government. I was very happy there and enjoyed the benefits of regular work hours and good wages. Almost as soon as I arrived I had tried to find a women's group and I called Bryony House to find out what groups were available. Finding that there were not any groups I realized that I really missed being part of the women's community. One thing led to another and before I knew it there I was back working in a shelter. I had a minor nervous breakdown the day after I handed in my notice in the government and accepted the job at Bryony House. What had I done! One shift at Bryony House and I knew that I had made the right decision.

Twelve years on I am still there and still passionately in love with everything connected with my work. Bryony House is a beautiful Victorian house which can house up to twenty-four women and children. Women can come and stay for up to six weeks. During that time they can decide what they want to do. Some may decide that they want to separate permanently from their partners and set up on their own. Some may decide that they want return home and try again. Some women are there for the first time and others have been there several times before. At Bryony House our role is mainly to give the women and children a safe place to stay. We offer information about what resources — legal, financial, housing — are available to them. We have weekly educational meetings where the women have the chance to talk about the violence in their lives and hear each other's stories. Staff do not put any pressure on women to leave or not to leave. It is totally their decision and we will support them whatever they decide.

For many women the primary concern is their children. At Bryony House we have child-care counsellors who spend lots of time with the children and are available to talk to the mothers about any concerns they have. The children generally adapt to life at Bryony House very well. They enjoy their playroom experiences with the child-care counsellors and sharing the house with many little playmates. The mothers, on the other hand, have to deal with the chaos of living in such close quarters with many other women whose lives are in similar crisis and who are struggling to make important decisions about their lives.

At times it can be pretty frantic but for the most part I think the women feel that their decision to come to Bryony was a good one. We know this from the many women and children who come back to visit us and who attend our annual picnic and Christmas party. I often receive letters from women who have moved away to other parts of Canada telling me about their lives, how they and their children have found happiness and saying how being at Bryony House had helped them break free from violent partners. Sadly, not every woman and child who leave Bryony House find peace and happiness.

For many women, being here is the easy part. They face many hardships setting up on their own. Poverty can be one of the main hardships and many will have years of struggle through the court system trying to get custody and maintenance issues settled. Many will be harassed and threatened by their ex-partners. Bryony House has an Outreach Program which tries to help women after they leave. The Outreach worker can offer follow-up supports to these women by meeting with them to work through any difficulties they are experiencing, accompanying them to court, and by arranging to have security systems installed in their homes. The Outreach Program also offers support groups where the women can receive emotional support by learning new skills and by meeting other women who are experiencing similar hardships.

I had a wonderful experience doing this job on two occasions when the Outreach worker was on extended sick leave. It was very different from working in the shelter, where you have the support of all the other workers and where once you leave another worker takes over.

The shelter is staffed twenty-four hours a day, both to take care of the residents' needs and to answer the 24-hour distress line. One of the great things about Outreach is that you can meet with women in their own homes and give them your full attention.

It would be difficult to work at Bryony House without the backup and support of the other staff. Over the years I have worked with some of the most wonderful women that I have ever met. Their love and friendship to me over the years is something that I treasure. I treasure too their love and commitment to the women and children who come through Bryony House, and their constant struggle to improve our services to meet the needs of all the women and children who use us.

I consider it a great privilege to have worked at Bryony House for all these years. I have gotten to know women from every walk of life, from many different cultures and religious beliefs. I am humbled by their courage in overcoming the sometimes insurmountable hurdles to break free from violence. I have learned a lot from them and I continue to learn every day.

All in all I can say that my years at Bryony House have been enormously rewarding. Every day is different, filled with fresh challenges and rewards. One never becomes complacent — it is very upsetting to see women and children arriving in distress but very comforting to see them settle in and feel at home. It is enormously rewarding to be outside somewhere and have women and children rush up to you with great warmth and affection because you had been part of their Bryony House experience.

I often think that my experience of coming to Canada would not have been such a positive one had it not been my good fortune to have been hired to work at Bryony House. No matter where I may go in the future, I share with many ex-residents that feeling that I too will always be part of the Bryony House Family.

Anne-Marie Woods

profile of an artist

My name is Anne-Marie Woods. I was born on January 10, 1968. I am the youngest of five children, Wendy, Louella, David, and Cherrie. My heritage is Trinidadian, but I was born in London, England, because my parents went there to study.

To me it was inevitable that I end up an artist, because my early experience was somewhat dramatic. My mother, as I was told, had to conceal me at the hospital where she worked in London, because they did not want married women training to be nurses. She tells me how other nurses covered for her with the lifting of patients, and worked her shift, until the time came that she had to be honest with the head nurse.

Because my parents were in England training and raising money for their other children in Trinidad, they were not able to keep me with them. So I was raised by my godmother, who I call Mom#2 to this day, and my godfather. They too were in England while my godfather studied, and my godmother had just lost a baby girl. I lived with them until the age of four, pretty much until it was time for us to come to Canada. Sometimes I wonder if it was hard on me, having two sets of parents, but my mom tells me I always knew who she was.

My childhood memories actually start from a very early age. I remember my crib, and for years I thought that my crib hung from the ceiling. Finally, after my last trip home to Trinidad I realized that it did not but that my godparents must have had a net that hung from the ceiling over my crib to save me from the evil mosquitoes. I remember my nursery school in Trinidad with Mrs. Dot and the many songs we used to sing. I also remember walking with someone holding my hand who must have been my godfather. I remember my green kitchen set and my Black doll Dana, whose hand I tried to stick in a socket once and got in a lot of trouble. I remember the times when I would visit my siblings, but I don't remember much about them — just being in a different house with a lot of people, and one night falling asleep with gum in my mouth and waking up with it everywhere.

At the age of four I remember being on a plane coming to Canada with my siblings crying and I just could not figure out why. Then we landed here in the dead of winter. Maybe they knew what long harsh winters we were in for and that summer in Canada would only exist in the month of July. I'm not sure what they knew, but they sure cried a lot. And that is how I came to be in Nova Scotia.

Culture shock

Now, let's discuss some serious issues like culture shock. My definition is taking a four year old from Trinidad and putting her in Miss Rose's Daycare. This marked the beginning of my childhood rebellion against European Culture. My rebellion started with the food: relish, hot dogs, Campbell's soup, and Kraft dinner were all foods that I never ate before but was expected to enjoy like all the other children that I did not look like in daycare. From there it only got worse; they wanted to throw me out for being disruptive and for telling the other children scary stories during naptime. While they kept me in daycare after a meeting with my parents, the next year I was off to Harbour View Elementary School.

At the tender age of five I learned what peer pressure was. The pressure to conform, the pressure to sound and act more like the other children in my school. Since I still had a West Indian accent and some of the words we pronounced were different, I learned at a very young age to assimilate.

Then, racism reared its ugly head.

Being the youngest of five, it was myself and my sister Cherrie who attended the same school together. Cherrie is five years older than me. Then primary children were in school a lot longer than they are now. So when my bell rang at 2:30, I would go to her classroom, sit quietly and wait for the big people's class to get out. One day as we walked home, there was something new in store for us. Some of her classmates decided that they would call her names and terrorize her.

This was probably the first time I heard the word "nigger." The second time was from a little guy who lived around the corner from me, who decided chasing me with chains was a fun event. The third time I was in grade one or two I believe and a family moved in up the street. Two brothers and a sister decided we would be their victims. They only lived up the street so Cherrie and I would be safe walking home until we got to about Albro Lake Road and then we would have to run home in fear each day.

Of course, as a child I didn't understand so they focused mainly on my sister, but I knew one thing. Fright. I knew that something was not right with these people calling us "nigger" and chasing us everyday, wanting to beat us up and threatening us. However, the straw that broke the camel's back was the day the younger of the two brothers threatened us with a knife outside our apartment door. If there is any reason for hatred to stop, this is why. I mean here we are two kids, age six and eleven or thereabouts, just trying to walk home from school and we have to live in terror; and a knife now come on.

After the knife incident our parents became involved, and all I remember is that my father went to their house and spoke to the parents and the kids. The parents were completely unaware of the goings on, and the kids, well, they just thought they were doing what they were supposed to. So we became friends, well, except the younger brother — he still held on to the hatred and never spoke, but our days of terror were over.

My sister Cherrie moved on to junior high, leaving me to handle the perils of the elementary school system all by myself. Now, in my school there were three other Black students, Sylvia, Colleen, and Michelle Colley, all of whom I am still friends with to this day and Sylvia is one of my best friends. It was in elementary school that I became a bully. I would say that my love for bullying and the arts both surfaced in grade three. Looking back, I think I decided to start fighting because of what I saw my sister go through and there were so few Black kids in our school it was an easy way out. Beat them up so that my differences no longer mattered. So in grade three I became a bit of a bully on the playground.

One thing about school that I always enjoyed was reading. I loved English class. So from a very young age I was always one of the top readers in the class. I was also very disruptive in class. As a matter a fact all my report cards pretty much say the same thing: Anne-Marie Woods is a good student but is constantly disruptive in class. If you can think of every way imaginable to make that statement then you can picture all of my report cards. I believe that it was in grade four at Harbour View Elementary School that I asked Mrs. McGinnes, my music teacher if I could sing to the class. The song I chose was, I thought, "I Honestly Love You," but now I'm not so sure. The response from the class was uproarious laughter. I don't even think I made it through the first line and I ran out crying. It was a horrific experience, but something in me persevered, and in grade five I asked to sing in front of my class on the last day of school. I proceeded to do that in every grade.

Grade five was an insightful year for me. I had a teacher named Mrs. MacRae, who I would say was not the nicest teacher in the school. It was here I learned what a reputation is. I still remember that first day of school with my funky book bag. I picked up my bag to put things in my desk and everything, and I mean everything, fell on the floor. I could not believe it. Then I heard it; "You may have gotten away with that foolishness in other classes, but you won't get away with any of that in my class!" I guess the teachers all talked about me (what a realization).

I was fighting a lot at this time. It seemed I was always on the playground with a circle of kids around me, cheering me on. I even tackled some of the biggest boy bullies in our school. I still have a scar on my right middle finger from swinging at Johnny Deyoung and missing and hitting the school brick. But a bully never cries, though my hand hurt like hell. I had to finish the fight and move on, which usually meant crying on my way home.

Imagine that, Anne-Marie Woods as a bully, but I had many positive attributes to me as well. I took in the little people, one of whom was Kari Jackson and believe me she was little. She was the littlest person I knew. Kari looked like she was in grade one when we were in grade six, but she and I became good friends on those long walks home.

During all of this time in elementary school, I continued to excel in reading and was cast as the orator in an operetta in grade five. I loved the school concerts where I could sing; I loved track and field — the high jump and the 100 meters and I won every year. I loved reading, so I knew that when I left Harbour View Elementary and headed over to John Martin Junior High School that things could only get better.

Junior High (the Awakening)

It was in junior high that a lot of things happened to me. I was having some serious problems at home and I released all of that in school. I stormed out of classes, threw books, etc. I just had no control over my temper.

I remember my very first day in grade seven English class. Jehad Chedrawy, the Lebanese boy I decided I loved in elementary, he was the closest to Black that I knew at the time. Well, Jehad kept hitting my desk. I told him to stop, then he hit it again. I said stop. Well, lo and behold he hit my desk again, so I jumped up, shoved his desk back and mine forward. Not exactly acceptable behavior in junior high, or anywhere else for that matter. So I got a detention on the first day of school. Then I got another one on day two in English class and then, yes, on day three as well. I seem to remember writing many many lines and having to read as well, but I came to like my teacher. The name escapes me.

In junior high I think I suffered from trying to assimilate again. There were a lot more Black students at this school. They came from Shannon Park, Notting Park, and even some from the Preston area, so I was very happy about that. However, I did not really fit in with the Black students at my school either.

At John Martin I was very active in sports from basketball, volleyball, ringette, track and field (where I tied the record for high jump), and soccer and even cheerleading. Now, here's something funny about a few of these sports. I could not really ice skate that well and could not skate backwards and I was scared to death of ringette, but I played it anyway. As for cheerleading, I asked my parents if I could be one and they said no but I did it anyway. I guess I can't really get grounded if they find out now, can I?

In junior high one of my best friends was Maureen Vaughn and I remember we went in a talent show and performed a mini show which I put together. Back then one of my favorite records was "That's Entertainment." Oh yes indeed old movie tunes. I put together a little number that started with "Me and My Shadow" (since she was white and I was Black, I was the shadow), then we launched into the Abba Dabba song about the monkey and the chimp, into "Show Me The Way To Go Home." I also sang a song with Marley MacDonald. These shows were a great way to practice the skills I thought I possessed.

Now, I would love to say that in junior high I excelled in music class. However, I was in the A class which meant we had to take music, and for one reason or another in Junior High that was not cool. None of the other classes had to take music. I think deep down I wanted to but some of the students in my class launched a complaint as it was not fair. Well, let's just say that the A class got rid of more than one music teacher. We just literally drove them crazy, like in the movies. The more out of control we were and the crazier we drove the teacher the better. We were always under principal surveillance. And we went through music teachers the way some people go through toilet paper.

Some very important things happened to me in junior high. I had my last fight, with Cindy, an all around jockette, who was bigger than most of us and hung with two of the toughest Black girls in Dartmouth. I'm not sure how it really came about but she didn't seem to like me too much. One day she called me out at recess time. Next thing you know I was mouthing off back to her asking her what she said? (I must have been deranged.) It ended rather abruptly with a teacher or someone coming out to separate us and, of course, send us to the office. It was here that I realized I had no rights. I tried to explain to them what had happened, and they explained to me that I was expelled. I think I was expelled twice in junior high, the other time was for swearing in the cafeteria.

Black History

I learned Black History. In my junior high days my brother, David Woods, started The Cultural Awareness Youth Group of Nova Scotia — an organization founded to foster cultural awareness, leadership skills and creativity amongst Black youth in the high schools. He started getting me to assist him at these events. So there I was watching debates, quiz games, and he started a theatre group called VOICES. I attended each of these events as an observer. Most of the participants were from the Preston area and they didn't know me, but they loved my brother.

Coinciding with this cultural awakening for me were the Natal Day parades. I still remember the first one I attended with my brother and the cultural awareness youth group. There was something magical about being part of a float with all Black people, music you could dance to, and just a feeling of unity. The best part of Natal Day was when we would swing around the corner leading to the duck pond. This was where the Black people started and never ended. It was the greatest thing — like being in a movie with all of your fans screaming and dancing. I still remember how it would feel when we hit the Black section of parade watchers. We might be tired but we would liven up our step. They were so proud of our float and we were so proud to have the support from the community. The parade would end the same way every year. We would party until the end, dancing with the float and then put down our signs and go to the natal day fair until the night time. Those were the days, I can remember it all as if it were yesterday.

It is very hard for me to explain what learning Black History meant to me, or now as we say African-American/Canadian History. Prior to learning this I was really heading downhill. I was fighting. I went through a stage where I tried to talk like a valley girl. I was pursing my lips together really tight and trying to get my jeans to fit me the way the white girls jeans did. I never understood how their jeans fit like that in the back. I tried everything, but I had a big butt like most young Black women and I just could not accomplish this goal I set out for myself. I even think I was a bit anorexic for a while and no one knew I was starving myself but me. I lost about twenty pounds by not eating.

Anyway, like a bright light at the end of the tunnel, Black history did something for me that is hard to put into words. When one grows up in Nova Scotia in an all white environment, one just accepts this as the norm. So, up to this point, most of my friends were white, I learned European history, most of the people I saw on TV were white. My teen idols were white, John Stamos, Shaun Cassidy, to name a few. That was my world. Suddenly, I was learning about African Nova Scotian History, I learned positive things about Africa not just about slavery. I learned of Black scientists and inventors. These things really changed my life. Prior to this knowledge every time we would learn something in school it would have a negative connotation. When we learned about Africa, we learned about slavery. When we did books they had the N word throughout them, thus reinforcing a negative stereotype in a system void of positive images of Africa or Black people. I'm not sure if this explains it but it's the best I can do at this point.

Here is an example of what I mean. I feel there is nothing wrong with having the book *To Kill A Mockingbird* as part of the curriculum for high school kids if — and a big if — if the youth in that class have spent time learning the positive things about Black people as well. If the youth in the class, White and Black, have an educational back-ground that was equal, where they learned of other cultures and not just European literature, history, geography, etc. The school system I grew up in was very one-sided. Having high self-esteem was difficult to achieve without ever having a Black teacher, or learning anything posi-tive that you contributed to society.

See, all cultures are important and the education system should make an effort to incorporate the true history into the books. However, as a Black woman I can only speak of what was missing in my miseducation. I brought up the book *To Kill A Mockingbird* because it was one of the books I had to read in high school. There is something about taking a book home to read that has Black people in it (for the first time), and they are referred to as "nigger" all through the book. There is something that makes this selection of a book even worse when, in addition to reading the book, you view the film and hear the word Nigger resound through your classroom. It's hard to describe this feeling but imagine if your entire life you never hear anything about your race unless it's negative, and you finally get to read a book in English that has Black people in it and the same stereotype is reinforced. Now, the debate I had later in life was that this is a great piece of literature, and that is how things were at the time period. I have to agree with that point, but from the stand point of an unequal education system, it is not the best choice. So, I am hoping that now in the new millennium that teachers are finding other books with positive role models from other cultures, that Black History is incorporated in the books and that there are more Black teachers. I know that there are more Black teachers, but it seems to me the education system still has a long way to go as far as including other cultures in their text books. Oh pardon me, was that a tangent? Well, I have to do that sometimes, I believe in education for all.

High school

High school really was, hmm, an interesting experience. I think I had some of my best times in high school. I was an active part of the Cultural Awareness Youth Group of NS (CAYG). Being a part of this meant being able to discuss and deal with all the issues I was facing in school as a Black student. It meant meeting once a week with other students like me. It meant exchange trips, the debating team, the quiz team, conferences, fashion shows, and the list goes on. I remember going to a National Black Youth Conference in Montreal, and the Youth and Race Conferences. There was always something for us to do.

My self-esteem and organizational skills skyrocketed, and all of this was done through an organization that was not a part of the education system. CAYG truly changed my life. I suddenly had a purpose, and I could express myself as a leader and an artist. Our group at Dartmouth High School held speaker series, fashion shows, dances, debates, etc.

Writing about this makes me want to cry. My brother started this wonderful organization that helped to mold me and completely enhanced my self-esteem. Words cannot express the influence he has had on my life.

CAYG was where I got to express myself as an artist. We had talent shows, dances and cultural shows all the time. I wrote several plays for the group, including a rap version of Twas the Night Before Xmas and a black version of A Christmas Carol. These shows were put on for the entire student body and were appreciated by everyone. The plays gave me a chance to combine creative and cultural expression.

I wanted a boyfriend but I was not the cutest in high school. Also when you are not giving up the goods, well, your high school relationships tend to be very short — a week to two weeks, maybe a month long.

I remember how one of my ex's told all his friends I was a virgin. It was like I was wearing the Scarlet Letter in reverse. I mean I remember UB40 came out with this song called Virgin girl or Version girl and all the brothers in the north end of Dartmouth would sing that to me as I passed by on the way home. Then to make matters even worse the show *V* came out — this awful show about aliens that came down to take over earth. That was it. I had a V on my locker, and Jerome Smith stood in the middle of the Dartmouth High School steps and yelled at the top of his lungs *"Anne-Marie Woods is a virgin."* Then because the sign of the V can be made with fingers like a peace sign that became my symbol. The thing is, looking back I think having the reputation of a virgin is much better than having the reputation of someone who slept around with every Tom Dick or Hairy man that came along.

I can't go heavy into the boys to men situation in my life because that's not an autobiography that's a novel. But I can say that coupled with my own willpower was a very effective contraceptive — it was called Reg Woods birth control. Reg is my father and the best birth control any young woman could have. All I had to do is picture what he would do if I ever came home pregnant and that made saying no very easy.

So somewhere in high school things at home for me were not the best and I tried to run away to my friend Chrissy Millar's house. I did it the same way they do in the movies. I put a bunch of pillows in my bed, packed a bag and left in the night. I don't think I lived at Chrissy's for too long before my parents found out where I was. I must have called one of my sisters and told them about my whereabouts. Not the best thing to do if you are going to run away.

I cannot remember the exact time lapse between running away and one day being kicked out literally when I came home, but I think it was all around the same time. Well regardless, I was no longer living home during the end of my grade twelve year. I moved in with my brother in Halifax, and finished off my year by not really attending classes, writing false notes and letting all my marks drop. It was easy for my marks to drop and to write letters because prior to this upset I was a pretty good student, so I knew if I got low marks in all my classes I would still pass.

The scariest feeling for me after the end of grade twelve was going back to read my marks on the wall of the school, to find out whether or not I would be graduating. I knew that I could have failed and I was scared to death. But there it was — I passed, I could graduate, not with the best marks mind you but I did it. I went to my high school graduation and I remember my mom was there, no one else. I'm not sure that any of my siblings were still in Nova Scotia, to be honest, they were all so much older than me, but Mom was there. I let her know that I was scared that I would not graduate and she said she had a feeling.

So now I was basically on my own having to find a job, and my brother helped me out, hooking me up with Rosella Fraser at George Dixon Community Centre in Halifax. I started out working the front desk and doing after school programs. It was here I discovered the gift I had for working with children. Mind you, I should have known that I loved kids before because I had about thirty babysitting jobs between the ages of fourteen and eighteen. This was just like babysitting on a larger scale.

During this time I was still actively involved in Cultural Awareness participating in rap contests, dance contests and talent shows. There was always so much for me to do, I was never bored. As a matter of fact I won the very first rap contest ever doing a rap called Oxanne, a spoof on the Roxanne Roxanne raps. And get this — MCJ and Kool Gee were in the rap contest. I believe back then they were called The New Beginning.

I was at George Dixon for about two years when I noticed that there was a group of children that did not fit into the daycamp or playground programs. It was at this point that I wrote my first proposal that I run my own program called Active Youth. Active Youth was a drama program for youth in Halifax's North End, and the beginning of my developing children's scripts. I am in the process now of getting Cindy's Shoe, my first real play, on diskette. It was the Black version of Cinderella and I still have the videotape.

Early in 1988 I received a call from Tony Bernard, Delvina and Kim's nephew, about auditioning for Four The Moment. Now, when I got that call I was not sure how to react. I had seen the group perform a few times and in those days I was heavy into the rap and dance scene. When Kim called sometime later, though, I was very excited but tried to sound calm and mature on the phone. I was twenty years old at this time.

I will never forget the day of my audition . . . Picture this. I was working full time and had no time off so I asked the ladies if they could come to George Dixon Centre. So there I am manning the front desk and the phones, and I have to take a break to go into the Kiddie Kapers Room so I could audition. From what I remember Debbie, Delvina and Kim were there and that was nerve-wracking in itself. Debbie Jones was the one I would be replacing. I think I sang "Somewhere Over The Rainbow" and a bit of "Amazing Grace" to see if I could harmonize and they were nodding and smiling. I had to keep running out of the room to answer the phone or deal with a member of the centre.

After that my life took a huge turn. I joined the group in May of 1988, and I went to see them in their final concert in Truro. It's hard for me to describe my life at this time. I joined the group at a time when they had released their first recording and I had approximately two months to learn their entire repertoire before we went on tour. Baptism by fire would be the words that best describe what I went through. My very first Four The Moment performance was that June at the Rebecca Cohn. We sang two or three songs; the two I remember were *Betty's Blues* and *Freedom Has Beckoned.* I was shaking from head to toe, while appearing calm on the outside. In my head all I could think of was come on Anne-Marie move, stomach stop, legs stop shaking. I was used to performing on my own, and this was an entirely new dynamic.

Now, here I am thirty-two years old, just over twelve years of singing with them, and I am preparing for our final concert to be held at the Rebecca Cohn on March 29, 2000. Funny, I just thought of the fact that we are ending in the very spot where I had my first performance with the group and many others since then. I look back at my years in Four The Moment and am thankful for everything that being in the group has taught me. I have traveled all across Canada, to Philadelphia, New York, and Germany. I have opened for Maya Angelou with them, met Oscar Peterson, and have had some very amazing and uplifting experiences. Some days, as I am preparing for our final concert, I find it hard to believe all that Four The Moment has accomplished, but I know that as the saying goes all good things must come to an end, while they still can be good. (I added that last part).

The same year I joined Four The Moment, I started university. I make it sound so easy don't I, starting university, but it was not. As it turned out there were repercussions for my actions in grade twelve.

I could not get into a university with my marks. I would have had to go back to night school to upgrade and take academic math. There was no way I was going back to high school. So I found out about the Transition Year Program, a program for Black and Native students. It was a chance for me to upgrade and attend university classes as well.

Since I was pretty smart and I had let my grades drop due to family problems, I passed the testing and was able to take two university credits instead of just one, as well as the pre-university math course from hell.

I made it through Transition Year without a problem, except with the math course which took me over two years to pass. The only reason I passed this course after two years of tutoring and extra help, was one, yes one, evening with Harvey Millar explaining the principles of linear programming and some other things. Then I finally passed with a 51 and was able to continue on with my degree and have my tuition paid for. I am forever grateful. After my first two years in university, I determined that I really did not like social sciences that much, and auditioned for the Dalhousie Theatre Program the summer of 1990. I remember that audition as well — it called for one contemporary and one Shakespeare piece. At that time I did not even know what contemporary meant. I found the *Merchant of Venice* because I remembered studying that in high school and I learned Shylock's monologue. I almost gave up, to be honest. I left the memorization till the last minute and just got scared and decided I couldn't do it. But something got me in there, walking up the stairs of the Dalhousie Arts Centre to territories unknown, and I auditioned and made it into the program. I graduated from university in 1993 armed with a Bachelor of Arts Degree with my major in theatre.

I have had many struggles in my life, and was on my own at an early age always having to fend for myself. It seems nothing has ever been handed to me on a silver platter. It's funny, though, people's perception of you — when they see you on stage or on TV, they think either you have money or you're stuck up, or you can't relate to them. I can tell you that I would not change any part of my life, even the hardest of times when I did not want to go on. I would not change them, the trials the tribulations, the heartaches the battles, the sadness, the suffering. I would not change it because it has helped to make me who I am today.

Today I am a 33-year-old professional performance artist who sings, acts, writes, narrates, does poetry (spoken word), creates, produces, and dances when my knees aren't too bad. For the past four years I have worked very hard at trying to make a name for myself outside of Four The Moment, making sure that people knew that outside of the group I was capable of my own success. Now this journey has not been easy. I was most recently told that I cannot sing by someone I both admire and consider a mentor in my life. I have been knocked down many times, and some of my projects were not well received. I have felt disheartened, discouraged and downright angry at times.

But there are a few things that have kept and will continue to keep me going. Number one is God. My faith in him has increased and I know that all things are possible with Him. He is always with me, guiding me, helping me to be strong, and to continue to believe in and accomplish my dreams and goals. The other thing is my love for arts, youth, and culture — the passion I feel for these three things cannot be surpassed. And there have been those people who have fully supported me from the days when I was Oxanne the rapper. There are people in this community who are following all that I do and have been there to lend a helping hand. There has been the repayment of seeing many of the youth I worked with going on to do bigger and better things or continue on with a career in the arts.

I have to keep my head up, stay focused and it's very difficult especially when trying to make it as an artist in Canada, let alone in Nova Scotia. I remember that in 1997 I applied for my very first Canada Council Grant and received it — over $15,000 to do an internship at Philadelphia's Freedom Theatre, an all Black theatre and theatre school. While there I was very lonely and wanted to come home. In addition to the loneliness I was not treated nicely at all; my credentials did not seem to matter because I was from Canada.

Once when working on the production team for *Cooley High*, I was assistant to the director, Walter Dallas. From the beginning of the re-hearsal process, the stage manager and I had a tense relationship. I'll be the first to admit I was completely out of my element on the production team, but I fought to get this position working on the show. Anything I could do wrong I did. I remember one rehearsal where I finally felt on top of the situation and I cued up all sound cues and music cues for Act II and gave the Act I tapes to the assistant stage manager to fix for me. I walked into rehearsal ready for the world and then the director says, "Okay I changed my mind. We're going to start with Act I." I wanted to die right then and there. I had to announce that I did not have those tapes. I then had to ask out loud in front of a cast of thirty-eight people and the crew if the assistant stage manager could please get me the tapes I gave to him. Time stood still. The ASM brought me the tapes, none were cued, I had to cue all of them thus holding up the rehearsal. All I remember is sweating bullets, I mean there was a huge puddle on the floor as I sat there cueing all the tapes and holding up the rehearsal process.

Things between me and the stage manager got worse, with us challenging one another during the rehearsals. Finally, when I'd had it with his negativity toward me, I reported him to the director and asked that we meet after an already lenghty production meeting. When the director asked the stage manager to stay behind because I had requested a meeting, he looked shocked. This was important because it was a chance to clear the air. After that we were cool again. I became more on point with my work, and an asset rather than a liability to the production team. About two years later that same stage manager worked for *Bring on Da Noise Bring on Da Funk* on Broadway, and he got me and my two cousins in for $15 each. We are still in touch and remain friends.

This story is a significant part of my life's history. Though I wanted to, I did not quit, I followed through. I was going through a rough time — feeling isolated and out of my element but I stuck with it, until I was an excellent Assistant to the Director. I never gave up, and ended up making great connections and close friends in Philadelphia. This story and many other situations are a model for how I want to continue this path God has chosen for me.

Good !!!!

I will not, at this point in my career or my life, let anyone put me down or hold me back. They can put me down all they want but I will not take any of the negativity in. I will always strive to do my best and trust in God and know that he has my back. ✓✓✓✓✓

I am at a turning point in my career, I believe. I plan to leave Nova Scotia in the next two to three months and head to Toronto, where I have recently signed with an agent. It is my plan to work in Toronto, to continue to develop my one-woman shows, and to get my face and name out there as much as I can. I plan to go full at it for three years. People have made fun of my choices, or they say girl you're still here, but that just makes me stronger. I will prove all those people wrong and I will make it just by attacking my fears face on and by pursuing the career I believe I am meant to have. Just by doing these things I feel I am already successful.

So, to anyone reading this, it's okay if people don't understand you, it's okay if people don't support you. Trust in God, keep the faith and even if your dream gets deferred for a while, stay focused and most of all believe in yourself. ✓✓✓✓

Linda Harpell
editorial contributor,
Street Feat – Voice of the Poor

,

You may remember seeing the television commercial for the pain-killer Anacin — a poll taken in a large town shows 77 percent choose Anacin over other painkillers. Well you probably don't know the name of the anonymous town. It was Orillia, Ontario, the town where I was born. I seem to have been in a hurry even when I was born. I was known as a "preemie," and made my mother give birth to me at the seventh month. The doctor on duty suggested that it was good that I was born prematurely as I may not have survived if I had stayed the full term in my mother's womb. Hmmm.

Anyway, I went home to live with my parents after my short stay in the hospital. My two parents did love me. For several years I grew up in a town outside of Orillia, a small community called Hawkestone. I was a serious tomboy. I liked being like my brothers. Now, I come from an eight member family: my parents, my four brothers, my sister, and me. I was a middle child in my clan.

Basically I was pretty happy growing up in Hawkestone. My parents being devout to their religion — a not too popular one (Jehovah's Witnesses) — raised us in the best way that they'd learned in their religion and that they knew. My parents loved me in their own way. I also learned all about the religion that my parents still willingly believe in. I felt happy during most of the time we lived in Ontario. I was a very quiet child. I didn't pick fights with anyone. I tried to keep out of trouble. You know what's been said, "You'd better watch the quiet ones . . . they've too much to hide."

One of the few flaws in my happy life came when my family and I had to visit my grandmother's home. Out there in Whittenburg lived my kind, sweet grandmother. She was a dear grandmotherly sort of woman. I did like her very much. However, whenever I went to visit my mother's mom, I also had to visit with my three great uncles who stayed in my grandmother's house. They loved me very much, too — in their own way. I learned from one uncle in particular all about giving and receiving a French kiss. I was paid for the experience. He handed me a five-dollar bill. I was very afraid of him and he seemed very big and scary to me. I was four years of age when I received my first French kiss. I did come to know all about "adult things" as I grew up. I tried to cope with the whole situation, but it got worse.

My mother suggested to my father that we move down to Nova Scotia so that we could visit my grandmother more often. "Because she may not be alive for much longer, and I do love her," my mother told my father. They talked it over and they decided in 1973 that we move to Nova Scotia near the small town of Stewiacke. I did try my best to deal with the further abuse that my uncles "lovingly" decided to give to me. I came to have more money than my brothers and my sister, for as I kept growing up, the price of their attention went up, too. They gave me five dollars, then ten dollars, then the money went up to twenty dollars each visit for the last few years.

My way of surviving was to split — what's medically known as MPD. The full term is Multiple Personality Disorder. The new term that the medical professionals use now is Disassociative Identity Disorder. Don't worry, I'm safe. I can assure you the only person I would ever harm is myself.

But there is more to me than just these experiences in my life. I've tried to learn as much as I could about about one style of communication that burns within me. I love to write, expressing myself with words on the written page. I have this flaming desire, this need, to write.

I even remember my first story — *For you, my Bonito!* It was about a young boy who befriends a wild black horse he names Bonito. Now his father, the owner of a small ranch, wants to kill the stallion because it is stealing the mares he wants to sell in the market. In the end the young boy leaps between the horse and his father just as his father pulls the trigger shouting, "For you, my Bonito!" I thought it was a very good story for a seven-year-old writer.

That story started me on my writing craze, which I've been hard at ever since. I feel really alive with the task of finding just the right storyline, the right words and style to express all of my thoughts and emotions. I love to share with the world everything about me. I've used different settings, characters, and situations to communicate to other people what I think about life. I wish there to be a sharing of our souls, of my spirit with others.

To achieve that result, I worked at doing well in school. It wasn't that popular when I went to school either. The other students seemed content with just getting by, however I felt good about all I learned in school. There's still so much to learn. I like the saying I once came across in my reading: "I do not know. Those words are the beginning of wisdom." I took the thought to mean that the person who is humble enough to acknowledge that he/she needs to learn more about a certain subject will be moved to learn more and enlarge his/her mind and become a fuller person. Wow! What a thought to consider!

In order to more fully learn, experience my life, and gain greater skills expressing myself both verbally and through the written word, I decided to enter university. Here is where my religious upbringing seemed to come out to hold me in check. An elder from the Kingdom Hall met with me briefly one night. "I heard you're thinking of going into university," he said in a kind voice. "I'm going to Saint Mary's University," I told him. "Oh," he said, "I expected so much better from you." He sounded disappointed with me. But I still went and even got my degree in English *cum laude* (with honours). This took place in spite of juggling my courses with my personal challenges.

Needless to say, I kept writing, especially longer short stories and novellas. I wanted to keep up my skills with all of my prose. During this time, I also had two relationships at two different times during my four years at SMU. They each came to an end after a brief time. I think that I grew from my experiences with those men. With all of my interactions with the other people at the university, my world expanded along with my desire to share everything I had learned. My life appeared to be getting better and better.

However, I had new challenges pushed at me. I began to . . . how do you say it? In psychiatric terms, I started to "shift." There were different young men in the university who would walk up to me and tell me what a wonderful time they had with me — when could we get together to have some more fun again? I was flat-out puzzled. They became confused with my response to them. I spoke quietly. "Please, don't be insulted, but who are you? And what was it that I did with you?" I really didn't know what it was all about. I was missing periods of time and during those times I did pretty wild things. A lot of my actions weren't "normal" for me. However, I did succeed at getting my courses completed and I did graduate.

Soon after university I managed to get a job at the Ferguson Library for Print-Handicapped Students. This library is at Saint Mary's University and I worked there for two and a half years. During this time my difficulties increased. I found it harder and harder to keep my life on an even keel. Everything came to a head, and I was told to get assistance psychologically and go for a leave of absence for mental health reasons or my employer would have to fire me. I chose to go for the help I needed.

I discovered through my ongoing therapy that the mental and emotional trauma I had suffered as a young child at the hands of my "loving" uncles did have long-lasting effects upon me. I did have to go for psychotherapy, which continues even now.

In the meantime, I came down with something that affected me physically. This was a big-time problem for me. I had complete numbness in my right leg and I had the dropsies as well. The doctors didn't think my difficulties were all that serious. I didn't either, for I had no pains with the problems that I experienced. After a few years of frustration and confusion, my neurologist gave me the iron-clad result of my MRI. "Yes, the MRI scan results show us that you have MS — that's multiple sclerosis."

So, I can safely say to anyone who cares to share a bit of their time with me, I am not boring.

Anne S. Derrick

lawyer

I have found myself thinking about my childhood. It wasn't that long ago although my daughters seem to think so. They can't imagine leaving the front door unlocked or driving without a seatbelt. It was a different time, growing up in a small essentially rural community, and, in the '60s, watching the Vietnam War on the television news.

My father wasn't home much. He was the headmaster — "The Boss" — of an all boys' school. I would often find him in his office or coaching rugby or track and field. He had one leg shorter than the other due to an athletic accident when he was a teenager and in the winter I would sometimes track him down by following his irregular footprints in the snow. I remember once my mother went away somewhere for a trip and I took my meals with my dad in the school dining room. My father had to braid my long blond hair before I went to school for the day. He wasn't very good at it and it all fell out long before the day was over. It makes me laugh now to think of my father, perched on the edge of my bed, balancing himself on his good leg, earnestly doing my hair, so out of his element.

But my father was not out of his element otherwise in his relationship with me. We were always close; he was keenly attuned to the injustice in the world and challenged me to question the way the world was ordered and be dissatisfied with it. It was understood that I would go to university and do well, academic mediocrity not being an option.

Even as a child I knew that not everyone had a good father. I had friends whose fathers drank too much and sometimes behaved strangely. But that was such a small insight into the world. Over the past five years, when I was representing survivors of abuse at the Shelburne School for Boys, I so often thought about the boys' school I grew up in and Shelburne, and the family lives of my clients as children and my life, and how cruelly different they were. My preadolescence, constructed as it was around institutional life, was so enriched by the school community. In the same era, many of my clients were being brutalized in the very settings where they were supposed to be safe.

It otherwise amuses me to think about my origins, the only feminist in Canada to have grown up in an all boys' school is how I style myself. I have a great fondness for all those boys who passed through my childhood and happy memories of my life as the Boss's daughter.

I have thought about all this more recently because my father just died. His connection to me was poignantly evoked by my mother's discovery in his wallet of an old black-and-white photograph of me when I was five. He must have had that photograph for years, all through the time I was growing up.

While he was gravely ill I could not deal with my memories of him and so I pushed them to one side and focused on the crisis at hand. Now that he is gone I'm letting myself remember him. He was such a splendid person even if he had no talent as a hair stylist. Toward the end my dad was relocated in the past at times, as evidenced by the fact that he commented with some dismay about my very short hair. He must have been seeing me as a young girl with long hair: when I told him I had cropped it years ago he admonished me to get a wig. Well, he had no one but himself to blame. It was his fault that I developed into someone who didn't care to impress other people and would make her own way in the world.

So even though I grew up in a boys' school, my adolescence was spent with women, first at an all girls' school and then at university. No one ever told me that as a girl there were things I couldn't do. Or if they did, I wasn't listening. I just assumed I would decide for myself what I wanted to do, or not to do, as the case might be. There was never any discussion in my family about getting married and having children: my privileged middle-class upbringing was intended to equip me to be self-reliant. From early on, I made a conscious choice never to get married. I was nine when I told Bob Oliver this: he was a track star at my father's school and I remember sitting with him at the edge of the sawdust pit where he was practicing his long jumps. I just told him, I was never getting married. I had other plans.

Being a lawyer was a natural choice for me, the girl who was destined to have a career and who had the advantages at her disposal to acquire one. I got the lawyer idea from a potted plant. It was in a lawyer's office, an apparently passive, and probably rented, feature of the reception area. In my capacity as the Student Union President at Mount Saint Vincent University where I was doing my undergraduate degree, I had to consult with a lawyer for some advice and that's how I met the potted plant that changed my life. That potted plant spoke to me of power and influence and I suddenly saw that power could be used to make a difference in people's lives. I was nineteen and I had figured out what I was going to do. I was going to get a law degree and then I was going to use the power of the law to change the world.

Since then I have never looked back. It hardly amounts to the visions of Joan of Arc but it is as close to a divine revelation as I am ever likely to have. Inspiration is sometimes just a matter of noticing that ordinary things are extraordinary. In my case, it was the Mount that gave me the opportunity to notice the inspirational potted plant. It is most unlikely that I would have been a student union president at a larger, more impersonal, male-dominated institution. So with good fortune and a little imagination I was able to figure out at nineteen what I was going to do with my life. I was going to get a law degree and make a difference. That was my plan: it will be up to others to judge how I've done.

I hadn't been a lawyer very long, just two years, when I got a surprise. I was pregnant. It was a shocking development and one I had painstakingly tried to prevent. Archie, my sweetheart, was thrilled at this completely unexpected turn of events. I was horrified but didn't do anything about it except brace myself for the impending end of my life. I can be a little prone to catastrophizing. As things have turned out, seventeen years later, my life hasn't been stopped dead in its tracks by motherhood. I now have a lovely clutch of spirited daughters, three in all, none planned, and a never-ending supply of life's treasures — beach glass, crayoned love notes, sticky kisses, and teenaged wisdom. And I am mindful always of the saying about how it's all gone before you know it: the fingerprints on the wall get higher and then they disappear. That children grow up and move on is not what I had expected to mind about parenting. Whereas I once couldn't imagine myself with children, I now cannot imagine myself without them.

It's been a good combination I think, being a lawyer engaged in public interest cases and being a mother. I have tried to bring my experiences of the gritty world of my clients and their struggles into my girls' lives. There is a lot of responsibility that goes with having a lot of privilege and Archie and I want the girls to understand that and, more importantly, do something with that understanding. I want my girls to be warrior queens. There are a lot of battles to be fought.

People who recognize me from my work as a lawyer are still often astounded that I have children. I am regularly approached in public by people whom I don't know and the observation has been made, if I am with my girls, that these must be my nieces. When I represented Dr. Henry Morgentaler in PEI I had to take Archie and our youngest with me as I was still nursing her. As they walked me over to the courthouse, the anti-choice crowd who were protesting outside shrank back as though they had encountered Satan. It was apparent from the expressions on their faces that they thought I must have got the man and the baby from the props department of the local occult society: they just couldn't be mine.

Being a lawyer has suited me just fine. That some people probably think I am a witch because of the cases I have done and the fact that I am a feminist doesn't concern me in the least. I probably am a witch — at least I always dress up as one on Hallowe'en when I go trick or treating with my devil children. I feel passionate about injustice and proud to stand shoulder to shoulder with my clients and their causes. I haven't found it easy: some of my own personality characteristics have made my career choice a challenge. I don't relish conflict and I am actually relatively shy. I almost didn't go to law school because there was a moot court (mock appeal) component of the second year curriculum. The idea of public speaking made me want to curl up and die. But I was determined to get a law degree and be an advocate and in the end, it is the court work and the advocacy that I enjoy the most.

I have known for some time that I have been uncommonly lucky. Getting to know so many people who aren't has sharpened my appreciation for my own life and its riches, my family and my friends, my education and my health. You just have to meet a few prisoners, especially ones serving life sentences, and even the most ordinary aspects of life acquire a special radiance — driving, looking at the stars at night, eating a sandwich in the sun, going for a swim, sleeping in your own bed. There is a lot I am very grateful for; there is a lot I haven't said. There is a lot left to do.

Amen!
say no more!

64

Lorri Neilsen

writer, professor

don't think of myself as heroic. Survivor perhaps. But a survivor in the same way as women I encounter each day are survivors. We keep our eyes open, we read the signs, we act, we connect. We commit ourselves to the work and the people who inspire us.

Allow me to tell you my story in multiple genres. I am a writer, a teacher, and a parent. I have often said that writing has saved my life. And I think this is true. As a young woman engaged to be married, I returned from a trip away to learn that my fiancé had committed suicide. I wrote my way through my grief. Confronted with immense challenges in my first years of teaching, I wrote my way into professional growth. Having lived through the challenges of a difficult home life as a child, I began at thirty to write my way into understanding, forgiveness, and a measure of peace. I write to think, to play with new ideas, to move myself to action, to connect. I write to understand my children.

And as a result, I use writing in my teaching to provide support to others, especially women, who sense the power of words to develop voice, agency, and their place in the world.

Early years

I believe every woman needs a mentor, a supportive friend, another woman — perhaps older, perhaps a family member — who has loved her unconditionally. For me, that woman was my maternal grandmother. I cherish my memories of Gram, but I regret not asking her to tell me her stories. When we are young, we do not always realize how important the stories are. We do not honour the wisdom of the aged in our culture. This is an early draft of a poem I am writing about Gram.

Glennie

The photograph is brown, and the
uniform is boxy, the ends of the nurse's
cap lifting, like origami wings, and under
the folds of the pages, I read: Glennie,
Strathclair. She is sepia here, but when I
think of Gram I think violet, mauve, I see lights
of a different shore, a life in mauve mists,
a husband dead at thirty-nine, two young
children farmed out — sent to a farm,
MacDonald's farm, no less —
and Gram, off to a hospital away away
where she could find work, find a path to the
rest of her life. I know so little, I stare at
the photograph, wait for it to speak.

Gram was small. I could hide her in my
arms when I was twelve. In my childhood kitchen
her laugh soared, she hooted and cackled. Her
cigarettes burned into tiny wasps' nests in every ashtray
in our house. She watched the Maple Leafs, tipping her
day's glass of stout — it's good for my blood, y'know —
and rocked forward at the edge of the chair, her fist
waving at a puck gone wrong. In her Victorian hand,
a curling dip flourish, Ethel Glenn wrote letters to any of her
twelve brothers and sisters still alive and when
I had left home, to me. We wrote about the
everyday, she sent a ten dollar bill
now and then, and I asked
after her health. Gram was
my forever.

I left at seventeen,
Gram went into a home,
her memory crumbling like
wet chalk, breaking into
bits my mother could neither
mend nor bear.

At my brother's wedding
Gram sat in the crowded church
In the sun motes float across a shaft of light.
She was alone among us, looking caged
in a withering body. Gram of the large laughter
and small feet and the whispers,
Glennie of days and nights and men
and women I will never know. Gram
of the cavernous chest, the shuffling, and the oyster
eyes. Gram of the mischievous glint,
the scent of lilacs.
Glennie, a woman who knew spring
as any woman knows spring.
And I never asked.

When I was twenty-one, I realized that I had lived in as many houses as I was years old. My father hauled milk cans from boxcars for CNR when I was born, and every move meant a small promotion, and so we covered the prairies: Winnipeg, Prince Albert, Edson, Saskatoon, The Pas, Dauphin, Saskatoon again, Thunder Bay. For my mother, a nurse who longed for stability, moving meant organizing the boxes and the lives of four children and one husband. Her only help was Gram, who lived with us for a few years. Just as we found friends, a church group, or learned the names of the neighbours in our new home, we picked up our belongings and moved on. I learned not to fear change. For me, the first born, each move was a fresh page, a chance to reinvent myself, an opportunity to learn new ways. I always fit in because I was invisible, quiet.

Learning to teach: Teaching to learn

I began learning about teaching at age twenty-one when I took a job teaching art, English, and French in Calgary in the late '60s. Since then I have worked as a public school teacher, a community college and continuing education instructor, a university teacher, a communications consultant, an industry trainer, and a tutor, among many other incarnations of "educator."

All my teaching, learning, and research are connected: as I teach in education, I learn about educative processes. I research teaching and write about that learning. The processes are integrative, inseparable. Teaching and learning with diverse populations has made me aware, in particular, of the need to attend to the many ways we learn and demonstrate knowledge. The university context does not always meet the needs of students who make meaning in ways other than writing and reading. As a result, my courses include opportunities for students to learn and demonstrate their learning using other literacies: visual and creative arts, performance arts, music, among others. These ways of knowing are often consistent with cultures outside the mainstream, and are often taken up eagerly by women of all cultures and contexts. Because the academic life is not always accepting of alternative ways of knowing, I was prompted last year to write this poem:

Scholar/ship

drydocked,
air where
water once ran,
wood split
shrinks in the sun,
sharpens into
slivers, points against
the light. The promise
of sparkling voyage dims,
dulling with the wash
of the tide. The hulk
sags, cannot sway,
does not dance, sees
only one grey
horizon.
Same rocks, shore,
hands, mouth,
voice.

Put me in the water.
This sere life
cracks my core,
bleaches my mark from
aging boards.
Dunk me into the
swell and I
will rise, will
rise, my arms
the sails inhaling
salty wind. I will dip,
dip, dive, will reach,
breathe crimson, breathe
azure, breathe saffron, and I
will paint
the sky

Women in education

For me, teaching and learning are not about control, about maintaining hierarchies, fostering subservience or blind devotion, nor are they about posturing or providing only entertainment. As a professional, I live the roles of advisor, partner in learning, elder, passionate explorer of ideas, and careful listener: I am uncomfortable when people think I have answers or authority. True, I must provide a framework for learning, articulate clearly my agenda and the reasons for them. I must learn to ask the right question at the right time. I must also support and encourage people to clarify and achieve their goals, help them assess their progress and make that assessment visible. But my primary goal is to work to create a community to which we are all responsible, to provide the context where everyone's contribution is valued. Everyone's. We all bring life and learning to this community. Risk, humour, challenge, and inspiration are hallmarks of such a community. We all learn from each other.

But finally, and always, I am the one who learns. As a woman, I am particularly alert to gender inequities in the classroom. I know these inequities; they are systemic. Whether it's the tendency for teachers to allow more air time for males in classrooms (all levels) or the use of discourses of competition (debate, one-upmanship, seeking a "right" answer), the inequities are played out daily. As I wrote in my recent book *Knowing Her Place* (1998), I was often silent in classrooms, did not believe in my own ideas or my ability to express them, deferred to others' authority and opinions, and, like many young women, tried my best to do the right and proper thing, whatever that might be. I usually did well in school because I was compliant. I regret this now. But like many women of my generation, I felt it was safer at the time to maintain the status quo. I didn't realize then that this is the mark of oppression: to go along just to get along. I didn't realize that silence is also a form of resistance.

Now, I hear stories daily from other women about their educational experiences. As a graduate student, for example, I learned much about my field, but I also learned about the political nature of the university classroom. I love to learn, and so I carried on, thinking I could help to effect change. This is a metaphorical piece I wrote for a brilliant doctoral student whose artistic dissertation was challenged by her institution. She had written a fictional piece and included her own art work. Some members of the university felt this was not "scholarly" work:

She came to the door and they asked
    — what do you want?
She answered
    — in, so that I may help. And because I am hungry.
They turned to each other, then turned back to her.
    — you may come in. Your hands look healthy. Your back is strong.
      We can find a place for you.
She entered. The room buzzed, she was electric with joy. Her heart beat as
      loud as summer.
One of them whispered to her:
    — turn that heart down. It's too loud for the size of this room.
By now, others had heard the heart. They began to whisper among
      themselves, wiss, wiss, hiss, hiss, and one by one their backs
      turned away from her and to their own work. She watched them,
      their dry and callused hands rubbing the same page again and
      again. Their fingers were blackened with ink. Their fingers were ink.
She approached two nearby, and tapped a shoulder. They turned to look at
her and she noticed, with alarm, that the pupils of their eyes were in the
shape of letters. And their irises were the color of granite.

She said:
    — please, I want to stay.
The two, Q and A, answered in unison.
    — then turn that noise down. It's very distracting. And give us
      your hands.
    Ours are tired.
She wanted a home and she was hungry.
What was she to do?

And below are the words of graduate students who found that the world of ideas and community of learners was not as equitable as they

71

had hoped. Most are women, but as is often the case, both women and men can experience inequities in the educational system.

> "And so there I am, in the front row, the dutiful little graduate student. The room is packed — there must have been a thousand people in that session — and I hear my story. My data. He is standing up there at the podium using my data, my examples, and calling them his. I didn't realize that being the star graduate student means you give away your data.
>
> "It's a laugh, really. He makes his reputation as this big critical theorist. But he refuses to stay in the university dorms with the other conference participants. He insists on a room in the Sheraton downtown, with access to a hot tub."

> "Oh, we were so frustrated. We revised and revised our writing and she became more and more abusive. The stories had to be just right. She kept reminding us what a big deal it was that we, as teachers, were publishing. But it was, finally, her publication, her name on it. Did she think because we were classroom teachers we didn't know that we were being used?"

> "He's telling every student he can that they need to work with him because he believes he's the resident expert in just about everything. So, like sheep, they follow. They want someone to take care of them. But the students don't know how thesis supervision fits into the academic market-place; they don't know the system. They don't understand he thinks of them as a commodity."

I recount these stories (modified, and with permission, of course) because I believe it's important to tell the back stories, the ones not usually sanctioned in our lives. Most of the general public believe that school is a safe and democratic place — public school, community college, university. It can be, but school is like any other institution: it's saturated with power relations. And most believe that universities are populated only with brilliant and ethical people. But let's face it — all educational systems are built on a notion of hierarchy.

Hierarchies breed competition, distort behaviour, co-opt even the most honourable of people into doing things they would not otherwise do: I live those contradictions, as do all my colleagues. Everything from testing to grading to accreditation practices in education reinforce competition. Low ability children are reminded constantly about their inadequacies, elementary school teachers are bullied into changing classroom practice for fear of not keeping up with Japan, or the school district down the road, or the demands of the market economy. Classroom teachers are forced by policy makers to do things the "right way" because right is best and best wins. In university seminars, the competition plays out in discursive hard ball — who has the citations and linguistic savoir faire to gain an edge in the conversation and win the favour of the professor. Each day, we try to find ways to undermine these practices. And so each day is a new opportunity for change.

But it gets complicated, too. Feminist theorists talk about the challenges for women in education — as public school, college, or university teachers. Students typically have higher expectations for us: we are supposed to be more caring, supportive, tolerant and flexible. When we are not, we are "cold, distant, unapproachable." (A man who behaves the same is "busy, overworked, businesslike.") We are expected to be giving of our time (even though most women teachers are torn between family and work obligations, and work the "second shift").

Like it or not, all of us hold women teachers to a double standard, including women teachers themselves: because we know the pressures on women's daily lives, for example, we tend not to ask for the services or extra help from support staff, secretaries, and others. We

73

tend, as Rosabeth Moss Kanter has said, to do our own "office house-work" in order not to make more work for our lesser-paid co-workers. Women tend not to "blow their horn," and thus we contribute to the belief that male teachers have more authority, and command more respect (who's in charge when the elementary school has a crisis? which gender do parents assume the principal is? why do university students assume our university president at Mount Saint Vincent is male?).

This is a poem I wrote years ago after working at another Canadian university:

Higher Education

You stand
across the doorway
of your wordthick office, and
give audience, nodding,
nodding. Just
so.

Middle-aged co-eds, frightened
by rumors of a desert Out There
wait to drink from your
tongue.

Your hard round lips
jut,
naked
from the soft beard.
Poised lips,
like your feet,
in position, just
just so.

> Elsewhere
> your wife, wrapped in a warm
> box, bathes your children, keeps
> your supper, puts
> her mind to bed.

O, patriarchy! the women
weep. It is not just. O, hegemony!
O, truth. No truth, no
justice. And so,
and so, nodding,
you give good confession
and they wail, touch
your wordbeads,
wipe their tears,
bless you for
your time.

Yes, justice. And
it is so. I close
my door to your altar, walk
to the window, watch
the moon. She sails over hallway gods,
drawing water, moving time. Just
rhythm, she is high and whole.

Teaching women in community

As much as possible I try to create a learning environment where students — in my work, they are often adults in mid-life — can learn without fear, without deference, and with the confidence that they will not be judged but supported and challenged in their growth. Twenty years of teaching has taught me that when adults enter university, they bring as much or more than they take away.

I learned about the transformational power of community when I began to teach. My first year was as a junior high English, art, and conversational French teacher. I taught a rough group of young motorcyclists who took up ceramics and black-light poster painting with an enthusiasm that belied their cool exterior. They loved art class and they supported one another. They became a community inside the walls of an institution that was otherwise hostile to them. We connected. They taught me.

I love learning, and I love writing. For thirty years now, I've been the student. I've learned as an actor in community theater; a writing consultant north of the Arctic Circle, inside a penitentiary, and near the tar sands of Alberta; a bank clerk and a grocery store cashier; a classroom teacher in elementary and junior high; a graduate student at the universities of Minnesota, Harvard, and New Hampshire; a visual artist, a potter, a technical writing teacher, a journalism instructor, a backpacker with a notepad, a mother, friend, lover, community worker. I've learned through writing books, articles, book reviews, scholarly pieces, essays, poetry, commentary in national and international publications about literacy, learning, writing, women, feminism and most of all, about qualitative research as practice. What connects the writing and the contexts are people. People with stories, people who make sense of who they are in the narratives we write together.

Life is inquiry, a practice of learning with others in as many contexts as we are fortunate to touch and be touched by. Learning is wild play: sometimes it causes tears, as wild play can do, but it grows hope, deepens our understandings of ourselves and others. In the academic world, where I now work, we rarely talk of the spiritual nature of learning, but it's there. We need to talk of it more. Learning waters the heart, and what grows is connection. And when we're connected, when we pay attention, we have an opportunity to transcend the differences that divide us. I believe this is especially true for women.

During the last ten years, I have learned much from the (mostly) women and men in courses and summer programs on campus, the Fundy Shore, off the coast of Australia, and in Ireland. What I know is that authority is not found in the latest theory or the size of one's curriculum vitae or the scholarly territory one conquers; it is earned in the simple practices of respect, of listening to one another, of being present. Authority is the ability to author our own lives, to write our own stories. For women, writing our own stories is a political act. Staying open to hearing each others' stories is the first step to changing our world.

ing open to hearing each others' stories is the first step to changing our world.

Here is one of my favourite quotes. It combines my beliefs in the power of community, of telling stories our own way, of bringing women together. It is an excerpt from "Can Mothers Think?" by Jane Smiley (In Brown, Kurt. [Ed.] 1993. *The True Subject: Writers on Life and Craft.* Saint Paul, Minnesota: Graywolf Press. 151 pages):

> . . . Nor do I accept universality, and its partner simplicity, as a concept. Nor do I any longer wholly accept modernism. What I substitute is a picture of many women in a room, exchanging anecdotes . . . all anecdotes simultaneously the same and different, the multifarious and the simple, the One and the many, existing together without cancelling each other out. To me that is the particular and complex vision of life that by and large is missing from our culture, whose absence has led us to invest our substance in religious fanaticism, crop monoculture, capitalistic gigantism, political and military conquest, aggrandizement of the self above everything and everyone else. It is a vision that, if we can insert it into the stream of literature, may help our culture to pause so we can save ourselves and the world that cradles us after all.

Wanda Thomas Bernard
A journey to self-determination

Introduction...

like to support people who dare to transgress and challenge the existing order of things, and I want to honor Carole Trainor's determination to be an educator who "is determined to make more profound meaning of women's lives." I am also proud to be among such great company with other women of Halifax who are committed to personal and political struggles. I am particularly pleased to share this space with my adult daughter, who is a trailblazer in her own right. For this brief autobiography I have decided to give you a glimpse of my early life, my education, my family, and my paid and unpaid work, which form parts of my journey to self-definition.

Beginnings . . .

I was the sixth of ten children born to Marguerite Slawter Thomas and the late James A. Thomas. I grew up in East Preston, a small Black community on the outskirts of Dartmouth. The biggest advantage I had growing up was that I was shielded from the ravages of racism and race oppression as a youngster. I went to a segregated school until grade eight. I remember having Black teachers and a Black principal, and all my classmates were Black. The leaders in my community were all of African descent. I had role models who looked like me, and it felt good. I did not feel different, or inferior, or marginalized. Does this mean there were not problems? Of course not! There were problems associated with socio-economic status and gender oppression. However, these all seemed manageable, and were effectively managed in the family and community.

My early school days were wonderful. I was taught to read and write before I ever went to school. My mother's godchild came to live with us when her parents died. She was about four years older than me, and she loved to play school. I was her student, and I learned well! When I began primary school, I was quite advanced, so my teacher gave me more challenging work. I loved Ms. Reddick, my first teacher and mentor. She is one of the reasons why I developed, and continue to nurture, my love of learning. I will be forever grateful to her for those early teachings.

I went on to grade one the next year, but only stayed in that class for two weeks before my teacher convinced the principal and my mother that I should go on to grade two. Academically that was the best place for me, but socially I was ill-equipped to handle the challenges that lay before me. I was a shy and introverted youngster and the placement with much older children only served to reinforce my social discomfort and isolation. As the youngest child in the class, I had to overcome many challenges.

Academically I flourished in the segregated school. I was constantly affirmed for my achievements. There was lots of praise and encouragement to do well and to always be the best that I could be. I remember reading all of the books in our school library, and the principal trying to find other ways to keep me intellectually stimulated. I remember having one of my stories featured in the school, and everyone talking about it. Those were very special experiences, and I would return to those early school days time and time again throughout my life's journey, during difficult and challenging times, when I thought I could not go on.

Despite my academic success, however, those feelings of isolation and sense of not really fitting in were to continue into high school, but for much different reasons.

Integrated schooling . . .

It was hard to leave the comfort of my community and school to go to the integrated high school in grade eight, but there was no choice involved. Even more distressing was my academic placement there. Those were the days of streaming, and I was placed in grade 8-A, the highest level. I was the only Black student in the class; the white students made me aware that I did not belong there, and my Black peers isolated me because they probably assumed that I thought I was better than them because of this *special* location.

I no longer fit with my friends and relatives, and I did not fit with the white classmates. I internalized a lot of the feelings of isolation and marginalization, and for the first time my academic work started to suffer as well. As I reflect on that now, I realize that my work suffered because I was trying hard to fit in with the Black students, and I believed that was the best way to do so. I wanted to be part of the "circle of friends" and felt that my academic location positioned me as separate from them. How does a young person reconcile such a dichotomy? I never did figure that one out, and my relative isolation continues today.

The one thing that did help me to connect was our collective challenge about the race oppression we were experiencing in the school and wider society. It was in the middle of the civil rights era and the Black students at our school were actively involved in the movement. I remember the historic visit of the Black Panthers, and the uprising at our school. I remember the day that Dr. Martin Luther King Jr. was killed. I remember the Black family meeting that led to the development of the Black United Front. These events, and reading the words of Dr. King and Malcolm X, being involved in the Nova Scotia Association for the Advancement of Colored People (NSAACP), and local events like the relocation of Africville and the Halifax Encounter Group, all helped me to develop a conscious critical awareness of race oppression, racism and the Black experience of Nova Scotia and other parts of the world. This was the beginning of my involvement in social justice work.

Early actions . . .

I remember a demonstration at our high school, challenging the racism we experienced from students and teachers. This led to the class action suit against the Halifax County School Board that the Preston area parents lodged with the Nova Scotia Human Rights Commission. This was a positive collective action. I believe that I was fifteen years old at the time. The monitoring of that work continues today.

I also remember attending a Black Family meeting at the North Branch Library. I think that I was sixteen and very conscious about the injustice that Black people faced in Nova Scotia. I remember voicing concerns of young people at that meeting (there were not many youth present), and demanding changes. The Black United Front emerged from that meeting.

I remember being part of a youth group in East Preston. I was the secretary and did not say a lot, but was quite active in the group. We struggled to bring the concerns of the youth to the attention of our community leaders and elders. The Recreation Association later developed from those early initiatives.

Critical Incidents . . .

When I think about critical incidents that have helped shape who I am, the first thing that comes to mind is my father's untimely death. I was twelve years old in the summer of 1965, the same year I began the integrated high school. On August 30 of that year, my father, my god-father, and uncle were in a tragic fatal automobile accident. My uncle was brain-dead and lived for eighteen months; the others died that evening.

It was devastating for all of us. My mother was left with eleven children to raise, nine of her own and two grandchildren; the oldest was eighteen years and the youngest was eighteen months. It was difficult for us to understand and comprehend what Dad's death meant, but intuitively I knew it was a bad thing to have happen.

But out of everything bad, some good does come. Because of Dad's death, we were introduced to many "helpers" and we also became more interdependent as a family unit. We learned to work together, to support each other, and to depend on each other. The helping tradition of family and community was made visible and clear to us, as people from many sectors helped and supported us over the years. One example of this helping tradition is the man who helped my sister and I go to university. There are many other critical incidents.

Gaining entry to higher education . . .

Even though there were challenges in high school about the quality of education that the Black students were receiving, there was no emphasis placed on higher education. Although I was a student who was doing well academically, no one in high school talked to me about going on to higher and/or further education.

That seed was planted by one of our community helpers, Don Denison, a white male army captain who had recently returned from a tour of duty in Ghana in West Africa. Mr. Denison believed that if we were given opportunities to go to university, we would make valuable contributions to the community. From the community of East Preston he selected my sister Valerie and her friend Connie who were in grade twelve, and me, from grade eleven, to go to Mount Saint Vincent University. He also arranged for students from the other Preston area communities to go to Dalhousie and Saint Mary's Universities. Mr. Denison went to each of the university presidents and argued for admission for each of us, and it happened.

Valerie, Connie and I were the first people from our community to go to university. What a mixed blessing it was. On the one hand, we had this incredible opportunity for higher education; however, it was also a challenge, as the entire community was watching us, some supportive and others waiting for us to fail. I was fifteen years old (remember I had already skipped a grade, and was going from grade eleven), too young to make life decisions for myself, yet entrusted with this opportunity that I might not have had, if my father had not died so suddenly. We were among the deserving poor of our community, because of Dad's death. Mr. Denison had returned to Nova Scotia shortly after Dad's fatal accident and was most impressed with my mother's ability to carry on with such a large family. He wanted to help her and saw this as a powerful vehicle to use.

In hindsight he was right. My sister went on to study nursing and health education. She now owns a home health care agency in Chicago, Illinois. Connie Glasgow went on to study education and is now a vice-principal at a local high school. I went on to study social work, later doing a doctoral degree, and now teach social work at Dalhousie University. Each of us also have children who have gone on to higher education, and we have been role models and mentors for many young people in our families and communities. Many others have not had the opportunities that we had, and as a result, I have devoted my life's work to making a difference for others, individually and systemically.

The other source of my passion for social justice and change is my own failure and subsequent desire to turn challenges into victories. Few people know that I actually failed my first year of university. That was a devastating blow to my ego and self-esteem, and the incredible sense of failure haunted me for years. I am now able to critically analyze the conditions that contributed to that failure, and this has helped me to understand that failing in one instance does not mean that one is a failure.

The intensity of those feelings of shame kept me from taking some chances in life . . . the fear of failing was too powerful. However, the gifts that came from that experience were the ability to face adversity, to face shame, to face challenges, and the incredible desire to succeed. I went back to the Mount after working "in service" at Dalhousie Medical School in the cafeteria. (Historically Black women could only get jobs in the service industry, cleaning in institutions or in private homes. We refer to that work as working in service, and a job in a cafeteria was also seen as being in service to others.) To serve medical students on a daily basis was in itself an incentive to return to university, because I knew that I did not want a life of work in service. From there I got the determination to do well, and a renewed sense of my own ability to do well academically. I began to believe in myself again, and since I returned to learning, I have not looked back. For example, I knew that a Bachelor of Arts Degree was not going to place me in a position where I could get the job I wanted. I knew when I went back that I would also go on to graduate school.

After graduating from the Mount three years after my return to school, I went to the Maritime School of Social Work (MSSW), graduating with my MSW degree in 1977. Nineteen years later, I received my Doctoral degree from the University of Sheffield in Sheffield, England. I am one of the first African Nova Scotian women, and certainly the first from my home community, to attain doctoral level education. One of my goals since completion of the doctoral degree is to demystify the process of postgraduate education, and to encourage others to pursue such goals.

Family connections . . .

Being part of a large family is a blessing and can also be an aggravation. The blessings are plentiful and, in my family, it has meant the opportunity to develop many authentic relationships across generations. My grandparents gave us legacies of hard work, spiritual direction, strength, and untiring hope. My mother has been an inspiration, and her devotion to her family never waivers. As a young widow, she could have given up on us many times as she faced the challenges of life, but she never did, and in addition to raising her birth children, she took in two grandchildren and a godchild. Her strength has been a beacon of light for me over the years when I found myself in darkness.

My mother was not able to pursue her dreams, because her father did not believe she needed an education. She had to stop school at grade eight, because her father refused to pay for her to go to school in the city and she had graduated from the segregated school. There is some bitterness about this, but I believe that my mother takes comfort in knowing that her children have all done well and have had many more opportunities in life. Mom has contributed to each of our successes in life, and does take pride in these accomplishments.

I feel blessed with sister friends who mean a lot to me. I have also been blessed with the privilege of helping to raise my younger siblings — that helping tradition started early on for me. When my father died, I began to help out at home, and at the age of twelve could easily prepare meals for the entire family. I remember going to schools to see how my younger siblings were doing, assisting with homework, getting them ready for school, and being a good listener when they had problems. For many, I was their second mother. These truly are blessings.

The aggravation came in the form of having many personalities to deal with, and competing needs. As one of the quiet ones, my needs always seemed to take a back seat. As one of the older ones, my needs were not a priority. As a doer and a helper, there was always a lot more to do than one could realistically manage, and my self-image got constructed around my *doing*. To challenge traditions and to change old patterns in family systems is to upset people who do not see the need to change. This challenge continues as I try to find new ways to be an individual, while staying truly connected in my extended family system.

On being married and being a mother . . .

I married young, at the age of twenty-one, just after I completed my undergraduate degree. My partner of twenty-four years is a wonderful person, and we have grown as a couple and as parents over the years. A gifted artist, George Bernard is the light of my life and the person I hope to grow old with. We are friends and committed partners for life. We enjoy a lot of benefits and unearned privileges as a heterosexual couple. However, as an African Nova Scotian couple, we also know intimately the experience of race oppression, which continues to be a daily struggle. We have experienced the sting of racism in every aspect of our lives. Our home had to become a refuge and buffer from the harsh realities of a racist and race conscious society.

We have managed to successfully negotiate troubled waters, and together we have raised a daughter, and have been a source of strength for his two older children. George was a father when I met him, but he was not with his children's mother. Their relationship did not work, but he always maintained some role in the lives of his older daughter and son. As a young stepmother I had to learn to develop and nurture those relationships, and was determined to dispel the prevailing myths about stepmothers. I encouraged George to spend as much time as possible with his children, and tried to help him develop authentic bonds with them. It is a blessing to have a positive relationship with both of George's children; these are relationships that developed despite the odds.

One and a half years after we were married, George and I had a child of our own, a daughter Candace. We only have one child together, but the three children share a close and special bond with each other. These sibling relationships did not materialize on their own; they too are the result of hard work and nurturing.

Being a mother that my daughter could be proud of is one of my greatest accomplishments in life. Candace was born during my senior year in graduate school, while on Christmas vacation. The pregnancy was easy, but labor and delivery were critical incidents in my life that have never been forgotten. Whoever said that a woman forgets the labor once she holds her child has lied. I have never forgotten the labor pains, and believe this is partly the reason why I never had more children of my own. But I have been an *othermother* to many community children.

Back to the positives . . . having Candace and seeing her grow to adulthood is one of the greatest blessings of my life. She is a wonderful daughter, who continues to make us proud. Getting her educated is also one of my biggest accomplishments in life, and has been a major challenge.

We put Candace in private school in grade primary, as her birthday was in December and we felt that she was ready for school at age four. She went to the public school for grade one and for the first time experienced racism, which had a devastating effect on her. I felt terrible because I had not prepared Candace for the racism she would experience in the public realm. She was subjected to racist name calling and derogatory remarks from her classmates, and the school refused to deal with it. Whenever we raised the issue of racism, her teacher insisted it was only a problem because we made it a problem. This was a typical racist response, to deny the victim's experience of racism.

The problem escalated when Candace stopped working and learning, and the school's response was to have her repeat grade one. I was determined to not allow that to happen. I knew how to fight the school's recommendation, and I challenged the decision at every possible level, and lost. This was devastating and horrifying. George and I decided to put Candace back in private school, because we feared for her future if the public school was to put a cloak of failure on her at such a vulnerable stage. The private school placed her in grade two, and we worked with her all summer to bridge the learning gaps. By December of that year Candace was working at grade level in most subjects and above grade level in reading. To say we were pleased would be an understatement. However, we were troubled by the reality that our class position allowed us to make this decision for Candace, while many other Black children who had similar experiences of racism in school had no such recourse. This led to another action.

We took our case to the Human Rights Commission, and won. Once the School Board heard our story again, in the form of a Human Rights complaint, they conceded and decided that Candace should be placed with her peer group in grade two. We refused to have her return to the public school and she continued in the private school until the middle of grade nine, when she chose to leave. This victory led to policy changes in the public school system. For example, parents now have the final say in regard to the academic placement of children, when the school recommends that a child repeat a grade.

The challenge to have Candace educated continued through to high school. There were many incidents of racism, classism and sexism that could have stifled her growth and her ability to learn. We met each challenge with a determination to win, not only for Candace, but for other Black youth as well. Candace explores many of these in her own biography. Suffice it to say that seeing her graduate from high school, then graduate from Dalhousie with her BSW degree on the Dean's list turned all of the fights into victories *for her* and *for us*. She is now coming into her own as a trailblazer, charting a different, but equally challenging journey as she launches her career in social work and education.

Trailblazing . . .

I have been called a trailblazer, not because I have done such wonderful things in my life, but because I have always used my position to resist, struggle, challenge, and to make a difference for others. I have been the only person of African descent in each of my workplaces since I began my social work career, and in each position, I have tried to effect change.

I first worked at the Nova Scotia Hospital, with adults, and later with children and families dealing with mental health issues. While working with adults I worked with a psychologist to develop a psycho-educational group for inpatients with schizophrenia. During my time on the children's unit I established a program for parents, and for community outreach, in recognition that in many cases the children's problems were rooted in their families and communities, and we were only treating the symptoms.

There were many times during my work history at the NS Hospital that I experienced racism from the staff and patients. I recall an incident where a patient refused to have me participate in the intake assessment. The psychiatrist refused to complete the assessment unless I remained. I later learned from the patient's family that he had only had contact with African people in a subservient role, and was not able to relate to me in such a powerful position. Apparently, his family had a "colored" maid. Another racist incident that remains a vivid memory is the reaction I got when I was first hired as a sessional instructor at the MSSW in 1984. The talk among my colleagues was that "the School must be lowering its standards" because there were two African Nova Scotian social workers hired to teach summer courses. I overheard the conversation, although I believe it was stated so that I could hear it.

I left the hospital in 1984 to take a position as a family therapist with the Family Services Association (FSA) in Halifax County. I worked throughout the county as a traveling therapist. I later learned that some people were uncertain about the decision to hire me, as the position had not previously been filled by a woman, and they wondered how a Black woman would be received in some of the more isolated communities. I loved the work and did well in the job. I was the first African Nova Scotian therapist to be hired by the FSA, and our referrals from those communities increased significantly. I co-founded a group for men who batter and a group for women who were battered during my time there, and piloted many family life education programs in the Black communities in Halifax County. I also developed and ran a support group for women at Bryony House for battered women.

One of the things that helped to break my isolation as the only African Nova Scotian social worker on staff at these various agencies was the connection to others through the Association of Black Social Workers (ABSW). I was one of four women who formed the ABSW in 1979, and am its current vice-president and coordinator of services. ABSW became the voice of challenge and a vehicle for change. Through ABSW, we were able to lobby for changes in social work education, policy and practice. I am proud of many of our accomplishments, although there remains much more to be done.

Community activism . . .

Much of my community activism has been rooted in my work with ABSW. This has involved a range of activities and initiatives, such as advocacy for changes in child welfare legislation and practice, and lobbying for changes in hiring practices. It has involved the development and implementation of anti-racism social work theory and practice in the MSSW and in agencies throughout the province. I have held leadership positions with organizations such as the Black United Front and the National Black Coalition, and have served as a Commissioner of the Nova Scotia Human Rights Commission. I have also been active in race equity initiatives locally, nationally and internationally. In recent years, my work has evolved to focus more on the intersection of oppression and the search for theories that affirm the realities of marginalized people.

If asked to name my greatest accomplishment in this arena, it would likely be the establishment of culturally appropriate services for African Nova Scotian clients, and the institutionalization of their right to have such services. Much of my community work is now linked to research projects that seek to bridge the gap between the community and the academy. I am able to use my position in the academy to directly link community needs with my teaching and research, which broadens the scope of my community activism.

From the community to the academy . . .

In each of the social work positions I have held, I have been the token minority, and in each instance I have challenged this position, while trying to use it to effect change. Joining the academy in 1990 was no different. I was the first African Nova Scotian to be hired in a tenure track position at Dalhousie University. This is not a position to celebrate without question, as given Dalhousie's long history I should not have been the first, but I was certainly determined to not be the last. As the only person of African descent in my workplace, I am isolated and often marginalized. It is a struggle to create an affirming space for myself in the academy and to effectively manage the competing demands on my time.

The interface with students . . .

(This section was published in an article entitled "Claiming Voice: An Account of Struggle, Resistance and Hope in the Academy" in the *Canadian Research Institute for the Advancement of Women Journal, 2000.*)

Students of color and First Nations students see me as a role model and unofficial mentor. They come to my office with stories of racism and discrimination, and feelings of isolation and marginalization. They are seeking advice, support, and assistance as they deal with very challenging issues, issues that impact on their learning. However, I have no real power to assist these students. At our institution, we have a committee that seeks to address systemic racism and discrimination, but it is limited by the absence of clear institutional policies and practices to deal with these.

Students of color and First Nations students also seek me out for supervision and other types of support. For example, I am fully deployed but frequently get requests from students for project and thesis supervision. These are not only students in my program, but students from other parts of the campus. I am in a double bind, as I understand their desire to work with someone whom they feel comfortable with, and do not have to "educate" as part of their educational journey. Yet, if I am fully deployed, and untenured, should I be expected to carry this additional work as a volunteer? I challenged this issue during the past year, and actually did get administrative approval for the additional deployment time to take on the role of supervising these students, a good example of challenging institutional practices.

In addition, students from mainstream communities who want to unlearn racism seek me out for additional guidance and support, often in terms of project or field supervision, to conduct workshops and conferences, or sometimes for coffee and talks. I am also frequently invited to speak in other classes on topics within my specialization and interest areas. These are all competing demands on my time.

Daring to transgress in the classroom . . .

I see myself as a progressive educator. I want and expect students to engage in their own learning. I challenge students. I expect students to be uncomfortable in some of my classes, as they come face to face with oppression and must challenge prior learning and teaching. I use incidents in the class, and current community and world events as teachable moments. I expect students to challenge me.

But there is a price to pay for speaking up and speaking out. For an untenured professor, that price may be tenure and/or promotion. I have had my work undermined in the academy. I have experienced a silencing of my voice and a devaluing of my experience inside the academy. I also have had the experience of challenging racism amongst white students, and to have this followed several months later by very negative teaching evaluations, which are used in future tenure and promotion consideration. In addition, I have experienced a "freezing out" and labeling.

I teach from a critical perspective, and know this is challenging for both students and teachers. I use a variety of teaching materials and pedagogical strategies to facilitate a conducive learning community in each of my classes. At times, hotly contested issues surface in the classroom, and I see these as teaching and learning moments, although they can be painful journeys for those most directly involved. Nonetheless, as an African Canadian woman, deeply committed to social justice, I must model respect for all voices to be heard. (I presented a paper called *Lessons from the Margins: Teaching Anti-Oppressive Social Work from the Location of Other*, at the June 1999 Canadian Association of Schools of Social Work Annual Convention, which further analyzes some of these themes that emerge in the classroom.)

Work load — the visible and the invisible . . .

When I first started teaching at the university, I had a reduced work load, in recognition of my specific location as the only, and the first, faculty of African descent. There was some recognition of the invisible work load I would be expected to carry. Within two years, however, the reduced work load was gone, yet the invisible work load and competing demands had actually increased, as I gained more experience. As professional schools and university departments deal with increasing demands and decreasing budgets, it is difficult for institutions to maintain the practice of reduced work loads for racially marginalized faculty in recognition of their invisible work, without institutional support for it.

I currently teach mainly in the MSW program. I was recently asked by an African Canadian BSW student if I taught at the school. This was a stark reminder for me that the majority of our most marginalized students are in the BSW program and, if not properly mentored, will never reach graduate level education. It has forced me to rethink my teaching responsibilities, and for the School to renew its commitment to increase the diversity of the faculty.

I continue to do double/triple duty. However, after some years of struggle and resistance, there is more of an effort to make my invisible work more visible, and to validate the significance of that work. Completing the doctoral degree has been a significant milestone. Yet, when I recently prepared for tenure and promotion, I was constantly reminded that there are many more challenges to overcome in the academy. The biggest challenge continues to be finding creative ways to bridge the gap between the community and the academy, in teaching, research and policy development.

Reclaiming hope . . .

As I reflect on my work in the academy, I realize one thing that keeps me here, and keeps me enthused about my work, is *hope*. Much of that hope comes from my community, from the struggle and resistance of my ancestors, and the hope that I imagined helped them on their journeys through very difficult periods in our history. They resisted with fewer privileges, resources and opportunities than I have at my disposal today, and somehow, those memories and reflections help me to put things into perspective.

I still work twice, maybe three times, as hard because of the demands from within the academy and the community. I have had health problems associated with stress. I struggle daily to maintain balance in my life, to talk the talk, walk the walk, and live to enjoy both. My spirituality is the anchor in my life. I have learned to say "I am not superwoman" and to believe it. I have learned to say no and not feel guilty. I have learned to delegate. I have empowered myself to assert my rights. I have learned to ask for help when I need it. I have learned to establish priorities and boundaries. I have learned that my silence will not protect me. I have learned to work with allies. I have learned to break the power of silence when it needs to be broken. I have learned that my experiences form a lens through which I see the world and interact in it. I have learned to appreciate all of my experiences, for struggle leads to resistance, and resistance enables me to reclaim hope. I have learned that sharing my experiences is also an act of empowerment.

Journey into the future . . .

Writing this brief autobiography has given me the opportunity to reflect on the past and look to the future. As I think about the political and socio-economic conditions in Halifax in particular and the world in general, I become worried. I see a growing conservatism and a repression of efforts aimed at challenging systemic inequality. I see a society that is less and less tolerant of diversity; however, this is more subtle than in the past.

The things that mattered to me as a youngster still matter to me — social justice for all is a life goal that I hope to see fulfilled in my lifetime, but seriously doubt that will happen. Until all of us are free, none of us are free. Until the dream is fulfilled, I continue the fight, but from a different arena. As an educator, my role is now one of getting others to take up the battle, and I see that happening more and more. And finally, my devotion to family and community and my spiritual connectedness, the anchors in my life, continue to sustain and support me when I need it most. I am grateful for the challenges and the triumphs and look forward to leaving others with a passion for social justice. If I can pass on this legacy to somebody, then my struggles will have been worthwhile.

For further reading:

Bernard Wanda Thomas (1999) *Lessons From The Margins: Teaching Anti-Oppressive Social Work From The Location of Other*. Presentation to the Canadian Association of Schools of Social Work Annual Meeting and Conference, Sherbrooke, Quebec.

Collins, Patricia Hill (1990) *Black Feminist Thought*, Routledge, New York and London.

Hooks, Bell (1988) *Talking Back, Thinking Feminist, Thinking Black*. Between the Lines, Toronto.

Moses, Y.T., (1989) *Black Women in Academia: Issues and Strategies*. Project Report on The Status and Education of Women. Association of American Colleges.

Erie Maestro

mother, librarian

My home country is the Philippines. I grew up and studied there. I came from a struggling middle-class family. I have three sisters and three brothers (a fourth brother died at birth). My father was a military officer and was often assigned to different places when I was growing up. My mother usually followed him and took the younger siblings with her.

My family had a heart mother who took care of the children, especially when my parents were away. We all called her *Nanay* which meant mother. We called our "real" mother Mama. Nanay came to our family to take care of the eldest child in the early 1950s and stayed with us till she died in 1993 at the age of 79. If anyone deserved a medal for unstinting love and selflessness, it would be my Nanay.

Nanay was a healer and a bone-setter. She taught us how to ward off evil spirits. She made our stomach aches go away, rubbed vinegar and applied special leaves when we sprained our ankles. There were times when she would bring us to another healer who could see images on melted candle wax and tell us what had brought on the unexpected fever. Nanay was quite well known in our neighbourhood and she never turned away anyone who needed her help. We were her assistants, ready to fetch the vinegar and the bandages. Nanay never asked for payments, but we would whisper to the "patient" to put something under the saucer of vinegar, so the pain that Nanay took away would not transfer itself to her. Did my family or Nanay distrust Western medicine? No. They all co-existed with no apparent contradiction.

So it was with other things. Since we all studied in private schools run by Catholic nuns or priests, we studied religion and the creation. In science, we studied evolution. No big deal.

In school, we were taught in English and were fined five centavos per word if we were caught talking in our native language. At home, our minds and tongues made the switch and we conversed in Filipino. There did not seem to be any contradiction. But we still watched the predominantly American TV and read predominantly English-language newspapers and comics.

And when I entered university, did my Christian beliefs clash with my attraction to and involvement in the nationalist movement, or the Left? No. If nuns and priests had no problems with it, why should I?

There was the tolerance for differences, the open-mindedness for possibilities and even for things that had no rational explanations at the moment. However, in the issue of struggling against the dictatorship, there was no staying on the sidelines.

It was the height of the nationalist movement when I entered the University of the Philippines (UP). UP was the state university and the premier seat of learning in the country. To be a nationalist was considered subversive and when martial law was imposed on the whole country in 1972, the reign of terror was even more pronounced. Fascism and repression under the Marcos dictatorship were not theoretical concepts, not when you were being chased by anti-riot policemen during a street demonstration or when word is passed around that your friends and classmates have been arrested and tortured. But the opposition knew how to stretch the limits and boundaries of martial law. I saw how people resisted and struggled at great cost. It was difficult to be a bystander; it was said then that if you were not part of the solution, then you were part of the problem.

In 1982, martial law struck home. My husband was arrested and severely tortured. For several days, his military captors denied that he had been arrested. When his parents and I were given permission to see him, I saw the marks on his body, which I later learned were burns from being electrocuted. My husband was rushed to a military hospital where he stayed for several days until he was transferred to the detention centre for political prisoners. Considered guilty until he was proven innocent, he was imprisoned for two years while undergoing trial for subversion. And during those two years, working for his release consumed me. I gave up my teaching position (the principal was probably relieved to see me go) and worked in a church-based human rights office.

As a human rights activist, I could work for my husband's release and visit him regularly in prison. At the same time, I belonged to an organization that fought for the release of all political prisoners and helped organize their families. We wrote countless letters and petitions, marched and shouted in the streets, demanded better prison conditions and visiting privileges, and supported our prisoners when they decided to go on hunger strikes. There were battles won — prison conditions were improved, visiting privileges were relaxed, the food budget was increased, and prisoners were sometimes released. The release of any political prisoner was enough to make all of the prisoners and their families hope that it would be our turn next time.

In 1983, I represented the families of political prisoners in a church-sponsored conference in New York. It was my first visit to North America. Before different groups in the US and Canada, I talked about the Philippine human rights situation and asked for their support.

In 1984, the dictator Marcos signed my husband's temporary release papers. In 1985, my marriage ended. It was a terrible blow for me. My work in human rights provided me with much needed comfort and distraction. My work now expanded to include the "disappeared," issues of the internal refugees, and nationwide militarization. In 1986, the Marcoses fled the country and another government took over. The human rights situation remained basically the same.

My ex-husband was arrested again in 1988. A friend phoned to tell me to watch the evening news on television. Have you ever seen your life flash inside your mind in a couple of seconds? I did. I saw a replay of what my life had been as a wife of a political prisoner. I broke down and cried. I never did like replays, in movies and in real life. However, I had no choice but to respond and help my in-laws again. I did what any friend would have done — searched for him in the military camps immediately, retained the services of a lawyer and made sure he got visits from his relatives and his partner. If things were different, I would have endured another detention but he was no longer related to me. I felt relieved when I could get out of this one. I heard he was given another temporary release after a year in prison.

I left the work with political prisoners and joined an ecumenical group that campaigned for the rights of church people, locally and internationally. Then I managed a women's centre that helped returning Filipino women from Japan — these were women who came back, distressed, broken and sometimes crazed because of what they suffered in Japan.

After several years of absence from school, I decided to go back to the University of the Philippines and study for my masters degree in library science. I was working as a library assistant in one of the university archives when I decided to try my luck in Canada.

That was my life B.C. — Before Canada.

Like most immigrants, I had to start all over again in this new country when I arrived in 1991. I thought my résumé was quite impressive. I got impatient when no one would hire me. Since I did not have Canadian work experience or Canadian credentials, I decided to do the honourable thing — apply for graduate school and finish my masters degree and hopefully, land a job. From Winnipeg, I travelled to Halifax and, after one and a half years, graduated with a Masters in Library and Information Studies (MLIS) from Dalhousie University.

My memories of those years in graduate school are ones of always rushing. My day started and ended with running to the daycare where my daughter spent her time, absorbing the English language in the smooth, efficient manner that all children have.

I would like to think that my daughter has always been old for her age. At age four, she would sit by my feet as I worked on the computer at the Dal Computer Centre or the Library Working Collection. She was happy surrounded by her books, crayons and toys. As she grew older, she came with me to the Immigrant Women's meetings, workshops and even my Spanish lessons at the community college. My daughter had her own after-school activities; then, it would be my turn to wait for her while she had her music, dance, judo, and swimming lessons. We used to joke that the time we spent on each other's activities would have qualified my daughter to become a member of the Immigrant Women's Support Association. I, on the other hand, would be an excellent dancer, swimmer, and judo student.

I had my child quite late in life. In fact, I conceived my child after my marriage failed. If only for this reason, I am convinced there is a God and it is a woman! In my seven years of marriage, I had believed that there was something wrong with me. Short of dancing before Saint Jude, the patron saint of hopeless causes, I tried everything that the doctors and the folk healers suggested. Massages, vitamin E pills, ridiculous exercises, and basal temperature readings. Who would have known that by losing my husband, I would get the child I had so desperately wanted? My family and friends welcomed my daughter, and stood by me as I raised her on my own.

These are some of the things that I feel strongly about:

Parenting

My child and I have to work between two cultures and these can come in conflict with each other. I have a lifetime of memories and experiences to filter what mainstream culture brings to me. My child does not have that. This is what makes cross-cultural parenting so important and challenging. How do I define cross-cultural parenting? It is raising my daughter to be proud of who she is and where she comes from. It is teaching my daughter the best of both cultures and thus helping her define her own person. It is also teaching my child that yes, race matters in this society.

All parents wish for nothing but the best for their children. As an immigrant parent, I always hope that teachers and mainstream society look beyond my child's colour and the shape of her nose and eyes and see her talents and her potential. As my daughter grows older, the fear and the worry never really goes away.

This brings me to the issue of racism. No child is born a racist. Racism is taught to that child. When my daughter leaves for school or for someone else's house, I hope that she does well and does not forget her manners, just like any other parent does. But then, unlike mainstream parents, I also hope that she will be treated fairly.

Four years ago, my daughter and I were subjected to racist slurs by a group of black and white teenagers while we waited by the bus shelter. It was a quiet Sunday afternoon. There was no one on the street who could have helped us. I had heard of swarming and these kids followed us, even as we walked away from the bus stop. They shouted, "Chink! Chink!" and mimicked Chinese sounding words. I was terrified. I did not know what to do, except walk towards the main road where there were passing cars. If anything worse was to happen, I told my child to walk up to the middle of the road and stand there until a car stopped to help her.

I still remember that incident and remember being violated. My child did not understand what "Chink" meant. She knows it now. She also knows what racist slurs are. We both have seen hate in other people's faces simply because they did not like how we looked. This is what it means to be afraid for our lives in Canada. That afternoon, we both had our introductory course in racism. This is the reason why the fear for my daughter never goes away. Mainstream parents may not worry about this, but I do.

I was not prepared to deal with it. Life under a dictatorship made it imperative that I learned how to survive. But it was escaping from gun-toting soldiers or plainclothes military agents. Not teenagers with so much hate in their hearts. This was something foreign to me. But I am learning. And I hope my daughter will be sharp enough to know it and strong enough to fight it.

Education and work

I have never taken my education and work lightly. Growing up, education was more of a privilege, rather than a basic right. It was a privilege to be in a private school, thus hard work and good grades were expected and demanded. True, it was largely a colonial education as I was growing up. However, in university, a whole world opened for me. I learned not only from my professors but also from the "teachers" outside the university walls — the workers, the peasants and those in the broad nationalist movement. A particular red painted slogan on the campus walls affirmed this: "*iskolar ng bayan*" (scholar of the people).

My colonial education (and I am not proud of it) and my English fluency have been useful in Canada. I am as good and as smart as anyone here. When everyone plays fair, then there is no need to think that one is being treated unfairly. Racism need not be blatant and violent; it can be very subtle. A black woman in a family magazine wrote that the very nature of racism made her feel vulnerable and tense. She cited the example of going to a store where the clerk is nasty and rude. She does not have all day to stand there and see if the clerk is nasty to everyone. She goes away not knowing if that clerk was just having a bad day or was a racist. When I read that, I knew what she was talking about because I also had been there.

I am a librarian and proud of it. I am passionate about my work because I believe that libraries make a big difference in the lives of everyone, including the newcomers to Canada. As a minority librarian (for lack of a better term, I will use it for now), I see their faces light up when they see me behind the desk. I look like them, I understand how they speak and I make it comfortable for them to talk in their halting English. I am certain that my presence helps to make them see the library as a welcoming place. And that is a good thing.

Socio-cultural issues

Children say the darndest things and my daughter is no exception. When she was in daycare and in grade primary, she made these statements and questions:

"You should not kiss, Nanay. You could get AIDS." How does one explain AIDS to a child? With a children's book called *Come Sit By Me* by Margaret Merrifield. We read it together and calmed her fears.

"Nanay, you have lots of friends who are girls. You like them very much. Then you are gay!" We had a previous discussion on what being gay meant when she had asked why there was a picture in a magazine of two men getting married. I had said then that people could really love each other even if they were both men, or both women, in a relationship. I remember that we did read *Asha's Mums* by Rosamund Elwin together after this remark.

"Nanay, what is RA-PE?" This was a new word for my child who was then learning how to read. She saw this word written on one of the placards of the women marchers in a demonstration protesting the atrocities against women in war-torn Yugoslavia. She had later drawn the demonstration and shared what it was all about to her grade primary teacher, who told me what happened in class.

I have realized from my daughter that children can learn to be accepting of differences, kinder towards other people and more aware of injustice than we give them credit for. My child and I are voracious book readers so it was so easy to enrich explanations with stories that dealt with these issues. When the words were difficult to find, the children's books from the library came to my rescue. It was so much easier later to tell my child that, yes, her friend's mother was HIV-positive or that her godsister was adopted and that her godmother was a lesbian.

As an immigrant mother and as a librarian, it is important that the books I give to my child reflect the faces and lives of different kids, not just white kids. It is also important that my child gets access to books that talk about social and political issues in the language and format that she understands.

When my daughter was four, she announced to me, "Nanay, I want my hair yellow." That was it — that was my wake-up call. Although I read to my child every night, she also needed the stories that celebrated who she was and other children who looked like her. A positive and good self-esteem needs to be built on and looked after. As my daughter grows older, she needs to know the history and the heroes of her first home-country. She needs to re-learn the first language which she first used to understand the world around her. As a young girl, she also needs to know and celebrate the work and triumphs of other girls and women. Not too long ago, my daughter asked me, "Nanay, what does TGIF stand for?" I knew that, so I replied that it stood for "Thank God, it's Friday." She laughed and said, "No, Nanay, it means Thank God, I'm female!" That remark was as good a report card as any.

Immigrant women's organizing

I am one of the founding members of the Immigrant Women's Support Association (IWSA), a mass-based organization of immigrant women in Halifax.

Organizing immigrant women is not an easy task. We are not a homogenous group of women. The immigrant women in Halifax, as anywhere else, form a diverse group. Even if we come from the same country and share the same race, religion and language, we have different class backgrounds and political beliefs. And immigration affects all of us in so many different ways. An immigrant woman summed it up very clearly when she wrote that if there is anything that determines the specific quality of our lives as immigrant women here in Canada, it would be race, class and language.

In spite of the differences among us immigrant women, we also have common hopes and aspirations, which include a decent job, a happy family, and good friends and of course, decent and affordable daycare. An immigrant women's network helps break down the isolation and loneliness that most immigrant women face.

As an immigrant woman in a workplace that is predominantly mainstream, I feel the responsibility of showing other immigrant women (as well as management and my peers) that we deserve to be in the workplace. It is important that immigrant women become mentors to other immigrant women, in and out of the workplace. I have not forgotten how I got here and how difficult it was to get where I am. And how stressful it can be to prove everyday (unconsciously and consciously) that I deserve to be here.

I believe that life will always be one of struggle and of overcoming odds. I believe in hard work. I also believe in fate. It gave me a daughter that I had always wanted. It also gave me back a long lost friend. After ten years, I met my friend from my university days in Halifax, the very same man I should have married but did not. In many ways, my life has come full circle, and continues on.

Terry March,
transpersonal therapist & philosophical counselor

My earliest memory is of paddling in a pink sleeper to an open bedroom window and talking to my friends — two lovely white birds who used to perch on the wide stone sill. Many, many years later when I asked my mother about that memory, she was astounded that I could remember so well the pair of rare white doves who nested in the eaves. She recalled once coming into the bedroom to check on me and startling the doves. I have many such vivid memories from the earliest of childhood, but this "first memory" stands out.

I also had many unusual sensory and extrasensory experiences, and still do to this day. For instance, I have always seen the world through a curtain of tiny multicoloured balls, and I don't mean in the metaphorical sense of rose-coloured glasses. And if that isn't odd enough, I have always "tasted" anything I've touched — that is, everything that I touch causes a taste sensation in me. For this reason, there are certain fabrics that I will simply not wear — nylon, for example — because they "taste" so awful. Foods for me taste different when I put them in my mouth than when I hold them. For example, chocolate's touch-taste is infinitely better than its mouth-taste.

These strange crossings of sensory experience also extend to vision and hearing. That is, certain sounds elicit simultaneous visual images for me, which appear a few inches in front of me, *not* in my mind's eye. Whenever there's a power outage, a microsecond before I experience a blinding flash of light much like a camera flash, which will wake me out of a dead sleep. The farther away the outage the dimmer the flash, comparable to the way lightning is experienced.

I have had such unusual perceptual experiences all of my life — I have synesthesia, which is a recognized neurological condition in which the brain appears to be cross-wired. With synesthesia sensory stimulation in one sense will also simultaneously evoke a sensory experience in another sense.

Synesthesia has given me a somewhat altered perceptual view of the world around me. This in itself has caused me to have a somewhat unusual perspective on things. It has also made me realize that any one perspective is very limiting, and that the rich diversity of people's perspectives presents amazing opportunities for expanded awareness. And that is why I have always found people extremely interesting, because there's always some wisdom to be gained from interacting with others.

Seeing the world through a veil of multicoloured balls can have its advantages, and all these unusual ways of experiencing seem to have given me peculiar aptitudes. For example, I seem to be able to assess people's state of health or illness fairly quickly. Not only that, but I seem to be able to accurately detect the area of trouble within their bodies.

However, I do believe that none of these wild and interesting ways of experiencing the world are of any use unless they are used somehow for the benefit of others. And that brings me around to how my life has evolved, because a central theme has always been working towards the benefit of others. I believe we have a responsibility to each other that goes beyond the obvious responsibilities of close social ties.

I have been fortunate to have had positive role models throughout my life who have inspired that commitment. My mother always helped others less fortunate. She did this without even thinking, it was a knee jerk reaction on her part. She was also deeply spiritual, although she struggled most of her life with the Roman Catholicism her Polish heritage thrust upon her. She had led a difficult life. In 1939 as Germany invaded Poland, Albina's family home was confiscated and the family was shipped to Siberia. Her 14-year-old brother Ted and her father escaped and joined the Polish resistance. But Albina, her mother and the two younger siblings stayed in Siberia, until the British Red Cross came and took the refugee families on a long journey down through Asia and into Africa, and eventually back up through India and finally eight long years later into England. There they were reunited with my grandfather and uncle, and immigrated to Alberta, Canada. And that is where she met and married my father.

My mother unfortunately died in 1990 from pancreatic cancer. But even in caring for her in the last months of her life she inspired me to train and volunteer as a palliative care worker. My private practice includes palliative and grief counseling.

Life was not easy for the Dutchyn family. We were very poor when I was young. We did not even have running water. My Ukrainian father had been raised on a large working prairie farm in Alberta. Having been born during the Great Depression, Father valued hard work and saved earnings.

When my parents moved to Ontario they initially lived with my maternal grandparents. I was born Tressie Ann Dutchyn, May 14, 1951, in Niagara Falls, Ontario, the oldest of five children. My maternal grandfather, John, was a significant influence in my life. I adored him. He was very philosophical and taught me many things, including the rudimentary skills of how to tie my shoe laces. He used to sit me on his lap and read the Polish newspaper from England out loud to me. I learned to read Polish before I could speak English. By the time I started school, I had somehow taught myself to read English as well.

When I was five, my parents purchased a small fruit farm not far from my grandparents. We moved several times until we finally settled in Queenston, in the exceptionally fertile region of Southern Ontario. Brock's Monument on the Niagara Escarpment stood guard over the farm. All the children were expected to work on the family's fruit farm. I was also responsible for housework, meals and looking after my siblings. Childhood was endless work and toil eight months out of the year. Summer was the busiest time of year on the farm. I came to look forward to the respite of school.

In spite of the earlier hardships I learned valuable lessons from the people around me. From my mother I acquired a commitment to the caring for the welfare of others, from my father I learned the value of hard work, and from my maternal grandfather I gained the love of learning.

I attended a Roman Catholic school and because I was bright, quiet and shy, became the darling of the nuns. I loved to read, wrote poetry and was an A+ student throughout elementary school. The school I attended had only two classrooms — grades one to four in one room, and grades five to eight in the other. From that tiny school I was plunged into a huge rural high school with more than 1,000 students, which went from grades nine to thirteen.

My high school had an unusual array of teachers, some of whom were retired scientists and university professors. The exceptional quality of the educators reinforced my love of learning. I became a member of the school's gymnastic team, and became president of the library society, which included working in the school's library. My most influential teacher was Mr. Johns, the guidance counselor, who also taught ancient history. He reminded me very much of my beloved intellectual grandfather.

Books were an escape from the drudgery of farm work. I also developed a passion for dance, and was fortunate to have a good dance teacher who was a bike's ride from the farm, so I was permitted the hour from my commitment to the farm to take ballet lessons.

Then at sixteen my world profoundly changed. I met a rebellious young man, three years my senior. Rob was muscular and solidly built — in fact he had been a goalie for the Dutch national hockey team. This man had an edge to him, and he was also severely learning disabled and could barely read. He drove a red sports car, he was wild, reckless and exciting. He was also immature with a quick temper. I became hopelessly infatuated, and with my infatuation all plans for university evaporated, much to the distress of my teachers.

We became engaged when I was sixteen and three years later we were married. His parents visited mine the day before the wedding and begged them to not let me marry their wild son. Unfortunately, I did not heed their warning, much to my later regret.

After we were married, Rob and I moved to Toronto. I held a number of positions and took a few university and college courses whenever I could, but Rob always had complaints about my going to school. He gradually became extremely controlling and threatening, sexually abusive and then when I became pregnant, physically violent. My family lived far enough away that they never knew and I was too ashamed to tell them. All of this culminated in a severe beating that landed me in the hospital, miscarrying at five-and-a-half months. Fortunately, my abusive husband left me and I returned to my family.

After several months I decided that I needed to start a new life, preferably somewhere else. Although I had always been terrified to fly, I decided the best way to face all my fears and start life anew was to do something totally different. I gathered up my courage and drove to the Air Canada employment office in Toronto and was promptly hired on the spot as a flight attendant. Three months later, after all the medicals and formalities were completed, I flew to Montreal to begin my new life.

I attribute my gutsiness to take risks and make changes in my life to my mother's influence. It was my mother who convinced my father to take a risk on purchasing a failing farm that in the end proved very successful. I could have chosen to hide from life and be fearful, which would have been perfectly understandable given the experience of my first marriage. Instead I took a chance on a new life by making radical changes, like moving to a different province and leaving my closest friends and family. Applying to Air Canada involved a risk that my application might be rejected. Montreal was a risk because it was far from home, it was a radically new culture, I didn't know a soul in Quebec. But the chance I took worked out for the best.

Montreal was indeed a change of scenery, and it had a *joie de vivre* that Ontario lacked. It was richly cosmopolitan and sophisticated without the stuffiness of Toronto. My self-esteem and confidence slowly returned. I was travelling to exhilarating European cities, vacationing in the Caribbean and Hawaii. I was discovering Canada and the US. I was meeting all kinds of interesting people, politicians like John Diefenbaker, respected writers like Pierre Berton, notorious writers like Xaviera Hollander, actors like Raquel Welch, comedians like Red Buttons, singers like Sylvia Tyson and Mick Jagger. Joe Cocker even asked me out on a date! But I didn't go out with him, since he had made quite an annoying pest of himself on the flight.

In Montreal I renewed my interest in dancing and joined Les Jazz Ballet Canadiennes when the company was first forming. In between flights I rushed off to the East Montreal studios, enjoying the intense workouts.

In Montreal I met and fell in love with a man twenty-two years my senior. Peter was also muscular and solidly built but that was where the similarity with Rob ended. Peter, in contrast to the abusive man I had been married to, was very gentle and mature. He also had one quality that has been a constant in my life — he cared about other people. He went out of his way to offer kindness even to strangers. We stayed together for almost three years, but unfortunately, Peter did not want to enter into another marriage and he did not want children. At twenty-five, I was ready for both. We couldn't come to terms with our differing needs and the relationship sadly ended.

When my relationship with Peter ended, another man, an angry man, took centre stage. Unlike my previous partners, Brian was tall and slim. But Brian was another man like my first husband — a man with an edge, a deep inner anger that exploded occasionally. He relentlessly pursued me, which at first was annoying but as I nursed the wound of Peter's rejection this pursuit suddenly appeared charming. I initially ignored the warning signs — the angry rages, the heavy alcohol consumption, the reputation as a womanizer. My friends were worried for me and I finally agreed that this guy, in spite of his charm, was serious trouble.

My plan was to quietly disengage from the relationship; however, when I told Brian of my plan over dinner, he completely took me off guard with his reaction. He dropped passionately to his knees and begged me never to leave him, but to marry him. I was so overwhelmed by his pain and what I interpreted as his deep love for me, that I agreed. I was back into a destructive relationship. We were married in 1977, moved back to Ontario and I gave birth to a daughter, Erin, in 1978. We settled in the historic town of Niagara-on-the-Lake, which was a few miles from my family home. Although I enjoyed my connection with all the people I met in my work, when I missed my daughter's first steps, while away on a flight, I decided to find work closer to home and quit my job with Air Canada.

By then I was very aware that my experience of the world was not commonly shared, and no one as yet had identified it as synesthesia. I was only aware that I was somehow different and that my perceptions were considered weird. I learned to be quiet about them, but found other ways of helping people. For example, by making them feel comfortable and welcome on the airplane, by actively listening as people opened themselves up to me, by becoming involved in their lives.

In the pursuit of trying to gain some understanding of my condition I was led to explore the paranormal, since what I experienced was certainly out of the range of normal experience for most people. I ended up not only taking a few more university courses but after three years of course work and study, I attained a diploma in parapsychology at the Institute of Parapsychological Studies, in Toronto. My exploration into parapsychology only gave me partial answers; I found that my experiences were even considered abnormal by paranormal standards.

I also found work as an administrator at Appleton Boys School, a residential school for learning-disabled boys aged eight to eighteen. I became somewhat of a maternal figure for the boys and grew to love many of them. I also slowly began to build a private counseling practice on the side.

However, on a personal level my relationship with Brian was not a happy one. In 1984 we moved to Nova Scotia, hoping to repair the marriage, but despite the support of ALANON in 1986 we separated. Once again in diversity I found something I could use to help others. As a result of that painful relationship, I used my experience to work with youth, counseling them through issues associated with their addictions.

I have always been committed to animal welfare and when I first moved to Nova Scotia I volunteered as an agent with the Society for the Prevention of Cruelty to Animals. Unfortunately, I found that the Society's policies contradicted their philosophy, so I left the organization. I then found work with a municipal recreation department as a fitness instructor. I had been looking for a class and none was available. However, given my background in dance, I was offered a position developing and teaching low-impact aerobics classes, which I did for a number of years until I went back to university full time. I also began seeing people as a counselor and established a private counseling practice in Nova Scotia.

A significant influence in my life was a friendship I developed with a woman who was living with a terribly abusive man. This man on one particularly horrid occasion dragged my friend and her children out of the safety of my home and I never saw them again. I was frantic for them, but there wasn't any help available.

When Second Storey Women's Centre in Bridgewater announced it was looking for volunteers to help set up a transition house for battered women on the South Shore of Nova Scotia, I immediately became involved. Eventually I was hired by the South Shore Transition House Association to do community education.

My strong work ethic surfaced and I committed myself to the cause with fervor: holding workshops with professional groups, junior and senior high school students; speaking to a variety of community groups and organizations on the issue of family violence; making countless media appearances; developing a kit on how to do community education on this subject; creating a booklet with a couple of senior high school students for junior high students; organizing and co-chairing a multi-professional association on family violence; chairing a volunteer organization that provided counseling to women in abusive relationships, and other activities.

The work also gave me the opportunity to finally begin to deal with my first abusive marriage. I would begin all my speaking engagements with my personal story. Painful as this disclosure was, the telling of my story also became a healing of those wounds and offered inspiration to others that life could go on successfully after an abusive relationship.

At the same time as I was doing this work, I discovered the strong feminist community in the province. I then became involved with the organizing of the Women's Action Coalition of Nova Scotia – a diverse group of women from all walks of life and professional backgrounds with a joint commitment to improving conditions for women in Nova Scotia. With the feminist community came an association to the lesbian community where I finally found and acknowledged my bisexual orientation. I subsequently became involved in a same sex relationship that endured for ten years.

The years from 1985–92 were years of major transitions and discoveries for me. I worked for Community Services and Family and Children's Services as, first, a social services worker then as a social assessor with the home care program. As well, my private counseling practice was thriving. I continued to be active in the feminist community, working towards improving conditions for women in general.

But something was deeply missing from my life. I confided in a dear and trusted friend, Kelly, with whom I co-facilitated an adult survivors of sexual abuse support group, that I would dearly love to attend university full time and complete my undergraduate degree. In the past I had applied to universities several times, been accepted into full-time studies but had been discouraged to continue by life's circumstances.

With Kelly's encouragement I decided to follow through with the dream I'd had since I was a teenager. I explored the options and settled on Saint Mary's University because it was a smaller university and I deduced I would be more likely to get lost in the large crowds of students at a larger facility like Dalhousie. I liked the homey environment of Saint Mary's.

After some helpful advice from Margaret-Ann Bennett in continuing education at Saint Mary's, I opted to take a summer course as my launch back to university. Margaret-Ann had recommended a philosophy course taught by Dr. Peter March, who she considered an exceptional teacher.

And so it was in the summer of 1992 that the next major transition in my life began. Margaret-Ann's advice was correct — Peter March was energetic, dynamic and had an obvious love of philosophy. With his clear blue eyes and his razor intelligence he motivated his students. I fell in love with his intellect immediately and, ironically, five years later I would fall in love with the man who galvanized my launch into university.

Although I thrived in university, winning scholarships and maintaining an A+ average, my personal relationship suffered. My partner considered my choice to go to university full time as an abandonment of the relationship and after ten years she decided to end it. That and the devastating loss of my dear friend Kelly to cancer two years earlier made life extremely difficult and challenging. I was faced with another major transition in my life.

In 1997 I graduated from Saint Mary's University, *summa cum laude* with a First-Class Honours in Psychology. I had been offered a research position at Wayne State University in Detroit working with a pediatric neuropsychiatrist. I had also been accepted into the PhD program in experimental psychology at the University of Alberta with a full scholarship. I opted for Alberta and moved there in the summer of 1997 to begin work on my PhD. However, after just a few short months, for a variety of reasons, personal and professional, I made the painful decision to withdraw from the program and moved back to Nova Scotia.

In the interim a friendship I had developed in university had blossomed into a romance, and Peter March became my partner. Back in Nova Scotia I took a year to rethink my life and decide what I wanted to do next. I resumed my counseling practice, wrote a number of columns and articles with Peter, and started attending the weekly philosophy colloquiums at Dalhousie University. I found what I wanted to do next — I wanted to study philosophy and to use that knowledge to benefit others, so I applied to Dalhousie, and was accepted into the special MA program in philosophy.

Peter and I started a joint column for the Halifax *Daily News*, entitled "Ask A Philosopher" in January 1999 and were married on May 23, 1999, at Point Pleasant Park in Halifax. I use the column as a way to continue to reach people, and to present feminist perspectives to the public. I have slowly incorporated philosophy into my counseling practice and am now a philosophical counselor.

I live in Indian Harbour, Nova Scotia with my three feline companions. I continue my commitment to improving life where and when possible both for myself and for others.

Cheryl Downton, R.S.W.

community social worker

My mother tells me she labored long and hard to bring me into the world, adding that my big head was cause for much concern. While the head was extra extra large and unable to be fitted for any infant bonnet, I suffered no medical abnormality. To this day, however, I am unable to find anything even resembling a hat large enough to cover my head. I've mostly come to terms with this reality, although I still sigh from time to time, when I see fancy hats on the heads of others.

As a very small child, I am told, I always needed to have my hands and fingers washed, not being able to deal well with anything gooey or sticky. Mom tells me I'd sit in my chair and flail my arms about with a distressed look on my face, and corresponding sounds of urgency emitting from parted lips. Apparently I was, even then, persistent, as I would only stop my protest once the offending substance was removed.

Growing up poor and with just one parent was seldom a concern when I was blissfully young and fiscally ignorant. I remember laughter and snow slides and childish games of hide and seek, and Mom hosing down our backyard lot to create a magical ice rink. That frozen paradise was the best winter had to offer — an opportunity to dance and dream and hope. I had a difficult time, even then, when things felt out of sync, like when the lower part of the ice rink was marred by neighbourhood dogs leaving their icy defined paw prints as indisputable evidence of their passing. Today, my sense and need for order is less rigid, although I remain, at times, unable to tolerate disorder and senseless chaos.

Still at a young age, I recall being fascinated and a little fearful of the elderly woman living next door. After all, she had the power to make lovely fresh donut holes, but not the donuts from which all donut holes must come. I also remember travelling to the local elementary school, not far from home, to play with friends in the school yard. My curiosity about how (and, sometimes, why) elements come into play and interact with each other led me to stick my tongue out to barely touch the icy metal fence post in the school yard. I knew from previous experience that my wool mittens would stick, so how about a human tongue? I'm sure I looked really silly, standing there, desperately trying to look unconcerned, my tongue tip attached to the unforgiving post. In what felt like long hours I was able to remove most of my tongue from the fence, as my own body heat had slowly defrosted the perimeter.

Growing into my teenage years, in conjunction with a move from small town to big city, my mother, perhaps fearful for my underdeveloped arts training, enrolled me in ballet lessons, piano, voice, CGIT (Christian Girls in Training), Girl Guides, junior, then senior, church choir. My mother's greatest joys then, and even now, were in the achievements of her children.

My adolescence was largely uneventful, although I remember long periods of uncertainty, dark moments of fear and anxiety, and times of great sadness. I continued to do generally well in school, although the accelerated math program was well beyond my grasp. Acting and singing (if only in the chorus, or as some minor character) in high school productions were both satisfying and emotionally challenging. Two class trips, one to Africa and Europe where a man in Venice exposed himself to me, chanting "You like? You like?" with my response a courteous (my mother would have been proud) "No thank you," and a speedy return to the comfort of the class group, and travel, by train, to Montreal for a student exchange trip.

My late teens and early twenties brought opportunities, largely through attendance at university and volunteer work, to meet and interact with a small number of older women. My deepened exposure to feminism and social justice issues moved from a raw, unfocused mass to something very real and, to me, a very integral part of my being. These relationships with women who had gained perspective through experience and study allowed me an advanced viewpoint and the benefit of their combined wisdom and courage.

Growing and experiencing led me to identify social work as a field of learning most synonymous with my personal and social justice perspectives. There followed a somewhat disappointing and disheartening course of social work education (patriarchy and misogyny were in evidence, yet voices of feminism and justice issues remained largely silent). Women of strong and strengthening voices were often ridiculed and attempts were made to exclude and silence us. One professor made it his mission, or so it felt, to minimize women's experience even to the point of refusing to entertain the reality of women's safety concerns when leaving the school after dark. Upon graduation I agreed, for my mother's strong sense of pride, that I would attend my graduation ceremony, something I had not done before. Even then I found that I could not conform to the establishment parameters, as I refused, much to my mother's chagrin, to kneel before the university president, instead inclining only my head toward him. Although now much more of a common practice, in 1984 it was almost unheard of.

Now in my sixteenth year of employment with a not-for-profit multi-service agency, I'm no more compliant than I ever have been when it comes to attempts by others to erode values, principles and bottom lines. It is not that I am inflexible or frightened of change — I'm always ready to listen and reassess, but I am unable and unwilling to dislodge those bottom lines that guide and shape me. I am pro choice, anti capital punishment and an ardent feminist. My steadfastly held view on giving, no strings attached, even if my gift is spit upon and thrown at my feet, troubles some of my contemporaries, yet I offer no apologies.

My work is mostly with women and families, with the occasional man requesting service. I offer counselling, therapy, advocacy, and trustee funds for those in receipt of Family Benefits or Income Assistance (welfare). My greatest joy comes from my client work, also the foundation for my greatest sadness and my boldest anger. Poverty, violence, abuse, terror, depression, uncertainty, and shame fuel my sadness, realizations, and new learning and ways of living, healthy choices and re-birth.

I bring compassion, honesty, respect, fairness and the combined experience of all with whom I've worked to my social work practice. Some of my strengths are my wisdom, analysis and capacity to engage with people, no matter where their starting point. The work crosses just about all boundaries, from violence to trauma, to sexual orientation, depression and emotional pain and suffering. My skill level and degree of expertise have been shaped, sharpened and enhanced by every person with whom I have ever worked.

While I have faced and continue to face many challenges in my life, as my own person, probably the greatest pain I suffer is that of a fat woman. Throughout adolescence and in my early twenties I battled with my weight (which, of course, means I was fighting with myself). To be a woman brings its own brand of oppression, and as a fat woman the oppression is twofold. There are not only the very aggressive and overt forms of fat oppression. The more passive and perhaps more insidious forms of discrimination can be found in stores, dressing rooms, public washrooms, telephone booths, hospitals, lawyers' and doctors' offices, banks, churches — all formulated to fit the "average" size and shape. Clothing manufacturers and food giants both exploit and oppress. Living as a fat woman in a world where women and their bodies are expected to conform to a thin and thereby lovable and valued standard brings hatred and, at the lower end of the scale, disdain and disgust my way.

There appears to be an endless number of characteristics which we attach to fat women — lazy, doesn't look after herself, slow-witted, exercises no self-control, ugly, unattractive, untrustworthy, mean-spirited, and so on. It is of value to note that fat men are often viewed as jolly, fun-loving, good eaters and robust, and although they suffer oppression in some forms, the overall toll is lighter. Of further interest is the manner in which fat women of color are not generally ostracized, hated and shamed within their own communities. Indeed, these women are characterized as caring, warm, ample, embracing, bold, and beautiful. This is certainly not to suggest that all fat women of color suffer no oppression, but merely to suggest different standards and a history rich with strong, capable, courageous women which translate into respect and reverence, again from within communities. The physical forms of oppression identified previously do, of course, affect men and women of color, as well as white fat women.

I no longer do battle with myself on any front, including over my size. I am, however, constantly and keenly aware of the physical barriers and oppression actively at large in my day to day work — do the chairs at the meeting place have arms? Can I park in an accessible spot? Are the washroom facilities adequately sized? Will I become trapped in a room whose only exit is easily blocked by others? When I arrive at the lawyer's office for the case conference, will I be able to sit in the reception area? Will I be able to sit at the end of the table so as not to impair the flow of discussion? Can I get aisle seats at the theatre? Some obstacles I have been able to eliminate, like my "no johnny shirt" position in hospitals and clinics and my refusal to patronize inaccessible public places, wherever possible.

These efforts can come with a tremendous cost and strain, both physically and emotionally. I challenge people who want to limit me and my attributes, attempting to define and confine me with their stares. I hold eye contact, I offer no apologies, and I don't back down, no matter the pressure. I find I need to remind myself from time to time that I am a good, strong and courageous woman who deserves my full support, as, infrequently, the stress, strain and fatigue reduce me to tears.

I have solid, caring supports in my life, in addition to Allie and Daisy, felines extraordinaire. My mom lives next door and we can thereby assist her as needed. Her finger joints don't work like they used to, her physical strength is failing, her memory is impaired, and she is not able to be as independent as she would like. My sister now lives in Pictou County with her partner, and I am glad she has returned from her sojourn in British Columbia — I've missed her. I have several good friends who take me as I am, with no apologies. Noreen, a Veith House colleague and long time dear friend and supporter, has made it a mission to run interference for me, when, for example, trips to hospital attempt to compromise my health and emotional well-being. She searches out the most accessible parking spaces and uncovers the most direct route to the specified department. She also reminds me when I am cranky and tired, overdoing it, and needing a rest. It is often Noreen's love and care for me that keep me focused and determined.

The future, at this moment, looks much like the present. I'll continue my work in all of its forms, be open to new and different experiences, and hold firm on my bottom lines. My life is generally a good one, and I no longer, as I did in my youth, pine to be made over into a boy and young man. No longer do I yearn for male privilege, as to do so is to wish to join hands with the privileged, to opt out of the struggle, the revolution. The work I can take on from within the ranks of women has the potential for a far greater outcome, with no apologies.

Maureen MacDonald

Member of the Legislative Assembly

've lived in Halifax off and on for approximately 20 years. During this time I moved to the Annapolis Valley for several years, and I have lived in the UK for a year or two while I was studying for my doctorate. Growing up as I did in Antigonish, this pattern of residency most certainly would not allow one to claim resident status; however, perhaps this is one of the wonderful things about Halifax. That a country girl who is not from Halifax could become the Member of the Legislative Assembly for Halifax Needham speaks to the warmth and generosity of many people in this constituency who can indeed trace their residency in Halifax's North End back multiple generations. It also says a lot about the shifting values and realities of many urban dwellers, whose considerations when voting for elected representatives extend far beyond "what's your father's name."

So . . . how did I get to this space and place. I think about this quite often, especially now that I'm middle-aged at forty-five years. As a social worker I guess I understand the importance of the early or formative years in one's life. I sometimes smile when I think about all the stray cats I begged to keep as a child, or how easily I cried at sad stories of lost teddy bears. I guess I have had a passion for justice and worthy causes for most of my life and from quite an early age. When I reflect on how I got to the place I'm at now, a member of the Nova Scotia Legislature, I realise the immense significance of the historical context into which one is born and the profound influence of teachers and significant care givers. In my case I grew up during a very important and exciting period of time for working-class Canadians and for women.

I was the first of three children, and was born and lived in rural Nova Scotia, Antigonish County, in the mid '50s, '60s and '70s. When I was three we became a foster family and I had two older sisters. My mother, who had completed grade eleven and had studied at the Normal College in Truro, gave up teaching after getting married. My father had left school in his early teens and for years he worked in lumber mills, travelling all over Nova Scotia, coming home only on weekends. Of course he also was unemployed for what seemed like long periods when there would be lots of tension and worry and he worked stevedoring from the port of Mulgrave, and collected "stamps" (i.e. EI). The first secure, decently paying job he had that allowed him to live at home was when he got on at the Gulf Oil refinery in the Strait of Canso. I was in grade eleven. My memories of my parents will always be how hard they worked to provide my brother and sisters with a good home, how much they emphasised work, education, religion and politics.

The poverty and hard work that shaped the lives of my parents as children and then as adults affected me at a very early age. At the time I was too young to understand the significance of my working-class origins. And frankly I never thought we were poor, because to a certain extent many around me were living in similar or even worse material conditions. I remember my mother often saying when someone (often herself) had to do without something, "Oh well, there's always enough food for the table, we never go hungry." However there was very little money for comforts or luxuries. We didn't have indoor plumbing until I was in grade five or six, or central heating. Many mornings in the winter I dressed for school by the wood stove and we could see our breath inside the house!

I attended a one room school house, just down the road, taught by my great-aunt (by marriage) Mary. She, my mother, grandmother MacDonald and several other female teachers had a profound influence on my desire to go to university. These women, each in her own way, encouraged me to read, to study, to speak up, to be independent. They were all very hard workers, active in their churches and communities, wonderful role models for a young girl in a world that was rapidly changing.

This was the period of expansion of the welfare state: hospital and medical insurance, family allowances, school expansion, student aid for university education, unemployment insurance were all programs of my youth. Sadly they are all under siege today.

I was in grade eight or nine when Trudeaumania sweep the country and like many young people of that generation I was profoundly influenced by the great social movements of the time, e.g. the Civil Rights movement, protest against the war in Viet Nam, and the students movement. In high school I was active in student politics, and my parents, who were and who remain staunch Tories, introduced me to political rallies and issues as a regular part of everyday life. The *Chronicle Herald* newspaper was an every day feature in our family as were radio news broadcasts. Influenced by my parents I began partisan political life as a "red Tory," suspicious of big government and big business, dedicated to self-help and local community control, and conscious of one's moral and social responsibility to those who were "worse off."

I entered St. Francis Xavier University at the age of sixteen, following the year of the student strike of '70-71. Student politics between 1971-74 was extremely interesting and I immersed myself in history, political science and sociology courses. I got involved in the student newspaper and I still remember the first piece I did which was on Father Topshee and the Extension Department and Coady Institute. I became active in X-Project, a program to tutor kids in local Black and Mi'kmaq communities, but I left the organization in frustration, though not before engaging in a struggle to expose the paternalistic and racist assumptions that informed a good deal of the project's work at that time. This was a very painful experience for me, but one from which I learned a good deal about respect for the cultural integrity of others.

I was active with the Progressive Conservative student group on campus. I remember Pierre Trudeau coming to campus for a huge political rally. Antigonish is a very Liberal area, and all the schools were shut down for the day and students were bussed in from all over the county. There was a question and answer period and I asked him what I thought to be a challenging and penetrating question from the floor of the Oland's Centre.

Trudeau took great exception to the question, as did the campus police who escorted me out of the gym. I think this was during the election campaign of '74 and the incident made the CBC national news. My parents were shocked. I was shaking in my shoes, but I remember thinking at the time that someone needed to challenge him. In hindsight I can't really believe I did this. After all he was the Prime Minister but I see it as a reflection of my deeply held belief of the need to have the courage of your convictions. It's no good believing something if you're not prepared to act on it. In that election I worked for the Stanfield candidate who really didn't have much hope as he was up against Allan J. MacEachern. However, I believe that election saw a greatly reduced Liberal majority, perhaps even a minority, with David Lewis and the NDP holding the balance of power.

Those were the days when students could still get jobs in the summer and go to university full-time with student assistance. After St. FX I was accepted into two very different programs, the Special Education program at Acadia and the School of Journalism at Carleton. I chose Ottawa and Carleton University, leaving Nova Scotia a Tory but returning very disillusioned by Flora MacDonald's loss of the leadership to Joe Clarke.

I worked in Truro at the Nova Scotia School for Girls for two years and while there decided to become a professional social worker. It was during studies for a Master of Social Work degree, when I had Rosemary Brown as a professor, that I became interested in the New Democratic Party. At that time she was a member of the BC legislature, during the Barrett NDP government. She is a remarkable woman, warm, funny, intelligent, passionate about racial and gender equality and human rights. She and the many progressive women and men faculty members at the Maritime School of Social Work would contribute to my political and personal development as a social activist. Of course, Alexa McDonough is herself a graduate of the MSSW and was a member of the faculty. However, she was not there when I was a student, and I did not meet her until she had been provincial party leader for at least a year or more. She, of course, is probably the person who has had the most influence on me politically, at least from the perspective of becoming a candidate for political office.

When I reflect on how much I admire and was encouraged or influenced by women like Rosemary Brown or Alexa McDonough, it still does not explain why I ran for political office. I think that the biggest influence on me in the late '70s and early '80s was the feminist movement. Being surrounded by friends who were becoming feminists gave me a peer group that would sustain my interest and commitment in working for social change. As so many others have written, suddenly we weren't engaged simply in actions to change the lives of others; we were engaged in working to change our own lives too.

It also was a movement that wasn't just about ideas. It was a movement that was about action, about concretely working to make change, and there were no sacred cows. We felt everything needed changing: who did the housework, how we had sex and babies, the kind of education we wanted and where we would get jobs — even language had to change. It really was a wonderful time to be a woman, and I guess it wasn't the best of times to be a man. This I imagine was especially so for those men who were in any way sensitive to equality issues, who by virtue of proximity and accessibility were the ones we could really nail!

When I was approached to be an NDP candidate I was quite young, maybe twenty-six or twenty-seven. I was working at Dalhousie Legal Aid as a community legal worker and we were involved in a very active anti-poverty agenda, organising around issues of housing, homelessness and tenancy, taking on NS Power for their credit and collection practices against the poor and especially single parents, challenging the small-minded Victorian welfare policy of the Buchanan government regarding single parents, mothers and teen moms.

The Minister of Social Services, Edmund Morris (a former mayor of Halifax and Member of Parliament) was the Tory MLA for Halifax Needham and the NDP wanted me to be their candidate. After thinking about this for a while I decided I would indeed run against Morris, and as it turned out Walter Fitzgerald (at that time former mayor of Halifax and former provincial Liberal cabinet minister, defeated by Alexa McDonough) was the Liberal Party candidate. It was a great campaign, and I got a big charge from saying, "It was a real horse race, me and two old mayors." Although I didn't win we had a wonderful campaign with lots of workers, a real coalition of people from many different activist groups. We came a very strong second and we used the campaign to build our organisational base.

I ran again in '88, which was a disastrous election for the NDP. Alexa almost lost her own seat. However, we managed to hold on, even marginally increase our popular vote and I again finished second. In '93 I was living in the Annapolis Valley and had just finished the first year of my doctorate when the election was called. I had become disenchanted with the NDP and electoral politics generally and played only a minor role in this campaign, working on election day delivering lunches to workers at the polls. This period was one where I really questioned whether electoral politics could ever result in the social change I desired, and I threw myself into doctoral studies and supporting women who work in transition houses to get unionised and to negotiate decent collective agreements. At that time I had decided to become an academic, to pursue job security and a teaching/research career with good pay, good benefits and good holidays, something I had not enjoyed thus far in my life.

What motivated my return to electoral politics was quite simple — years of Conservative and then Liberal governments, free trade agreements, the assault on social programs, and the deliberate implementation of fiscal measures causing poverty and unemployment to grow. The federal election of 1998 gave me hope that electoral victories were possible for democratic socialist candidates. In 1998 I had completed my PhD and had been on the faculty of the Maritime School of Social Work for not quite two years, when Russell MacLellan called the election. I had already been nominated, following a five person contested nomination for the Halifax Needham constituency.

On election night, March 26, 1998, I was elected by a landslide, defeating a Liberal cabinet minister who had been my successful Liberal opponent in 1988, ten years earlier. The euphoria of the NDP win that night, nineteen members, a tie with the governing Liberals, and the largest number of women ever elected in one caucus (five) was a wonderful experience. I tell people the highlight of that evening for me wasn't winning my own seat; rather it was when Yvonne Atwell won her seat in Preston. Yvonne is a wonderful, warm, wise and generous woman, with grace and presence and humour. However, this joy gave way to great disappointment when eighteen months later our numbers fell to eleven, and three women, including Yvonne, lost their seats.

I would not be telling the truth if I were to say that it has not been difficult adjusting to life as an MLA. The hours are extraordinarily long, the issues complex, the needs and demands many, and the resources to provide solutions limited, especially if one is not in government. Nothing in my life could have prepared me for the loss of privacy and for the objectification of one's persona as a politician. Because I still see myself through my own experience, which I find to be quite a normal and natural life, it is very hard to understand why some people would react to me as if I am "special" or "important." To me

I'm just me, so becoming the persona of MLA has been a challenge. At the same time, and at the other extreme, it is hard to understand why someone who I have never met before, who knows little or nothing about me, can trash me as someone whose only interest in life is advancing my own interests at public expense. Politicians have acquired a most unflattering public perception which applies to us all, whether it fits or not.

Political processes are also very gendered. I have had to bite my tongue more than once, not an easy thing for me to do, when some member of the public says something extremely sexist. It's even tougher when it's given as a compliment. Like the man who called me up to talk about user fees in the schools shortly after I became the Education Critic and ended our conversation by telling me he watched me on Legislative TV and found me to be a "feisty little darling." What do you say? There isn't a male MLA in the world who has had to contend with such flattery, I'm sure.

Would I do this again? Absolutely! I love this work. As far as I'm concerned I have the best constituency in the entire province. As I say whenever I have a chance to talk about Halifax Needham, it's a very unique place. We make ships and beer in my constituency. We also make music, art, film, video, and music. We are home to Africville, and the spirit of this historic African Nova Scotia community is kept alive by former residents and their descendants. The first public housing in Canada can be seen in the beautiful Hydrostone area, where following the 1917 Halifax Explosion, the Halifax Relief Commission set about with city planners, providing for the rebuilding of Richmond. There is more social housing for seniors and families in my constituency than any other in Nova Scotia, provided both through public housing and co-operative housing programs. The largest complex providing extended and continuing care for seniors east of Montreal, Northwood Manor, is in my constituency. There is a military base, Stadacona, and the dockyard. Halifax Needham is home to many non-profit organisations, such as Stepping Stone, Mainline Needle Exchange, Adsum House, Phoenix House, Veith House, St. Leonard's, the Black Business Initiative, Hope

Cottage, L.E.O., Ward Five Community Centre, the Black Workgroup Cooperative, the Brunswick Street Cooperative, the Black Educators Association, Parker Street Food and Furniture Banks, as well as the Mi'kmaq Friendship Centre and Head Start programs, the African Canadian Employment Centre, the North End Community Health Centre, four of the five designated inner city schools, some of the most interesting and social justice orientated churches in Metro, the North End Parent Resource Centre, and *Street Feat, The Voice of the Poor*, and many, many more. Agricola Street itself is a wonderful landscape!

I figure if visions of grandeur or power start to dance in my head, I have plenty of people, organisations, and places in my constituency who would only be too happy to remind me from where I come and what the "real" issues are.

I don't know how long the good people of Halifax Needham will want me as their representative. I do know that as long as they want someone who believes the role of government is to place the fundamental needs of the most disadvantaged and vulnerable citizens at the top of the priority list, then they will find in me a very willing servant. I've had quite enough of governments who are only too quick to use public resources to placate the interests of the Sobeys or the Michelins. What's good for General Motors isn't always good for all Nova Scotians. For me this means government must pay serious attention to the desperate plight of much of rural and small town Nova Scotia, Cape Breton, aboriginal and Black communities, seniors, especially those with very low and modest incomes, and other low-income groups, people with disabilities, single mothers and their children, the chronically unemployed and underemployed. The policy issues therefore must be sustainable economic development and employment, education, income security, enhancing social programs such as health care, promoting equity — breaking down barriers to equality of opportunity and finally guaranteeing sustainable financing of public services through fair taxation policy.

In my activism over the past twenty-five years I have come to see history as an on-going struggle between the powerful few and the less powerful many. I know absolutely that I will always be politically active in the project to redistribute social and economic power in our province, country and internationally from the few to the many, whether it's inside a political party as a partisan or in the community as an individual player or member of a loosely knit or a more structured group. Right now it's as a partisan. This isn't necessarily easy work nor does it necessarily win you a lot of friends or give you personal fortune or job security. It is however personally very satisfying to know that I do have the courage to act on my convictions and that I am trying my hardest to respect and honour the trust placed in me by my constituents.

Julie Godwin

working at home mother

When my son was born, I knew I was a witness to something bigger than myself. I was in awe and terrified. I had no idea how to be a mother. My own upbringing mixed with society's expectations was not the recipe I wanted to follow. What makes a good mother? If I read to my child every night, join the PTA, attend every soccer game, ensure he maintains straight A's, and bandage all his boo-boos, will I then attain good mother status? How could I possibly live up to these images? The answers to these questions have not come easily. It is a lifelong process. In order for it to evolve I had to go back to my beginnings.

Much about my own birthday remains a mystery. I was born near London, England, in 1962. I was adopted at six weeks old. I know a few facts about the circumstances surrounding my birth; however, the intimate details and the poetry are missing. What should have been a time of elation, celebration and wonder was blemished with the negativity of shame, guilt, and secrecy. My elaborate fantasy life served well to fill in the missing pieces. This was a tremendous help at the worst of times.

Perhaps many people do not care to know the details of their beginnings. I feel the need to know. I have no idea what time of day or night I was born. Was it warm and sunny on that June day? Was it a long labor? I certainly remember all twenty-seven hours of my labor. Was my biological father involved? Did they let her hold me before they took me away? Were there any family members or friends around her for support and comfort? Did the doctors and nurses show kindness and compassion to a frightened teenager?

I remember my own experiences in the hospital, some of which were far from supportive or respectful. Birth is a profound experience every time for all those involved. It is a time of great vulnerability for the birthing mother. She is completely exposed, relying on those around her for support. It is a courageous act even though it happens all the time. It deserves immense respect.

In many ways birthing has become routine and the magic has been replaced with technological efficiency. I sometimes felt absent from my experience of giving birth. There was an unnatural clinical feeling to it which came from all the control and orderliness. The negativity I sensed in those vulnerable moments left me feeling unsure of myself and of my responses. Too much control left me feeling powerless.

There was one caregiver, whom I felt truly had respect for childbirth. Her voice could put me at ease. She was a true coach who kept me focused on my own experience and did not try to tell me how I should feel. With some of the staff I sensed indifference — as if they had a cup of coffee to get back to and I needed to hurry up. I should somehow follow their schedule and not my own. It reminded me of a factory. Push it out and move on to the next one.

I so admire those caregivers who have not lost their admiration and respect for the birthing experience, the ones who do not bring their judgements into the moment. Whether a woman is rich, poor, prominent, young, white or of color, these factors should never negatively affect this process. I suspect my biological mother did not escape discrimination in her situation. It was the early '60s in a conservative Britain and she was an unwed teenager giving up her baby. It was a situation ripe for harsh judgements. It saddens me to think how she must have felt. I am quite certain there were no flowers of congratulations on her nightstand.

Quite a few women came through the ward where I stayed with my newborn son. I was there for eight days and had many roommates. The ones who stood out for me were those women who were young and unmarried. The older, married women were treated much better overall. Some of the nurses were subtle in their discrimination. They could be so cruel without being too obvious. A smile through gritted teeth or a later than usual response to the call button. Questions were sometimes answered with a tone of impatience. If you peel away the layers and have a closer look at the beliefs that foster this behavior you can see a disdain toward certain mothers that is not just localized to the childbirth experience, but everywhere on a daily basis. Society's image of mothers is not necessarily the truth. I now realize that it was not me who did not belong; it was the system's belief that did not belong in my experience. This realization affects me on a daily basis in regards to my own mothering.

After I was born, I was placed in foster care until I was six weeks old. I know nothing of the strangers who looked after me until I was adopted. My adoptive parents were told they could not have children. This must have devastated them, for having children was what married couples did. Adoption seemed the only alternative. They adopted a boy a year before they adopted me. It turned out they could have children of their own and my sister was born three years later.

We were now a family and everyone had their roles to play. My father was head of the family and the provider. He was a very strict man with many rules. He expected obedience and had tight control over everything, especially his family. When we stepped out of line, the punishment was harsh. Threatening us into good behavior was common. This was very difficult for me because from birth it seemed I had my own rules.

I was a handful, so I've been told. I did not like to follow schedules. I was the first one up in the morning and the last one to want to go to sleep. I had enough energy for all of us. I had much to say on every subject and constantly wanted answers to my questions. Sitting still was difficult. I had always felt like I had landed on the planet at a full run. To be submissive was horrible for me and I was punished regularly when I did not conform. "Children are to be seen and not heard" was a phrase I heard often. We were never to talk out of turn or to even speak at the dinner table. I so wanted to make my father proud of me and to have him love me. Who I was seemed too much for him. My fiery spirit seemed to enrage him often.

It is very difficult to talk to my mother about those early days. She is uncomfortable talking about her feelings. Like most mothers she wanted to be a good mother, but that is difficult to do living in an environment full of such rigid rules. I am certain she started out with the best of intentions. She did not like to upset my father. Her role was clear just like her mother before her. I often wonder if she questioned or felt she had the right to question her role as wife and mother. After all, she was provided for and had children to raise — what more was there?

As a woman and a mother, I have seen external changes in attitudes since my mother's time. Women are no longer tied to the home, nor, it would seem, are they expected to be. I cannot count the times I have been asked, "So, what do you do?" upon meeting someone, only to have an awkward silence follow when I tell them, "I am at home." Even those I know fairly well feel the need to ask if I am doing anything else yet — as if my life has no real meaning. I could not possibly choose this for myself. There must be something wrong with me.

I find myself dreading these questions and responses from others. It would seem easier at times to keep it a secret. To stay at home does not mean I cannot do anything else or have nothing else interesting to do or say. It does not mean I have such low self-esteem that I do not believe I can achieve greatness. Staying at home does not mean my life lacks excitement. It is not the lowest rung on the ladder of success.

To now choose what we as women were expected to do for so long is a bitter pill to swallow for many. It is not considered a lofty goal, nor is it profitable. Just look at what we pay our child-care workers. We have more respect for athletes in this society. Child rearing is exciting to me, certainly not every minute but neither is every NBA game. Excitement comes from how I perceive my life and what meaning I derive from what I am doing. It is hard for many women to see this choice as exciting and rewarding when they are bombarded with shame for having made such a choice. Why is it the years spent mothering look empty on a résumé? Is there no real skill needed or acquired? It is time to change our perceptions of mothers and mothering.

Our family left England for Canada when I was almost five. We sailed over on a ship called the *Corinthian*. My first visual memories are of this journey. We came over in May when the weather was still quite cold. The trip was at times frightening. I still remember what it felt like to taste corn on the cob for the first time and to look over the side of the ship at the immense ocean. I felt so small. I felt a comradery with my father. It was the only time I remember feeling that way. We were the only ones who did not become violently ill. We got to wander and explore the ship. We landed about a week later and took a train from Montreal to Winnipeg where we took up residence in a huge old house, which we shared with a family we had met on the ship. Eventually we moved into our own house and it was there that my life took a turn for the worst.

I truly believe it was not just career that influenced my father to move to Canada. My mother's family was not fond of my father, particularly my grandmother. She really disliked my father as well as me. She wanted them to take me back to the adoption agency. She was a force my father had difficulty dealing with. Two very controlling people at odds constantly. Coming to Canada was a way to separate from my mother's family permanently. But coming to a new country with small children and no support is not an easy task. The pressure to succeed was overwhelming. Although we made friends quickly the effects on my father were great. His drinking increased and he loved to party. I remember being frightened by the late night arguments and getting in the middle of them when I thought my mother was in danger. My insecurities about family and belonging increased. I had been told that my biological family could not take care of me so my parents adopted me because they wanted to love me and take care of me. Any further questioning was met with vague responses. I began to wonder what all this meant.

My mother took on a job to help out. It was around this time that my relationship with my father changed. The sexual abuse, I believe, began when my mother worked nights. Nothing would ever be the same again. All of this special attention, as he called it, made me feel like dying. I wanted him to love me but I also wanted to be invisible. I was a child who had a boogey-man who was real. I lived in terror. Something was horribly wrong! I became withdrawn and felt despair and hopelessness. My curiosity about where I had come from increased. I believed I was being punished just for being me. Perhaps my birth was a terrible mistake. God must really hate me. Maybe, if I tried even harder, I could make things right.

By the time I was ten we had moved to New Brunswick. My mother and sister took a trip back to England for three weeks. It was during this time that I told my father never to touch me again. It was the bravest thing I had ever done. The sexual abuse ended but abuse continued in other ways. My anger grew. My questions about my beginnings were mostly left unanswered. I was given a few facts and was made to fell guilty for asking — as if I was ungrateful to my parents. They loved me — why would I want to know more?

Even through all my feelings of worthlessness I knew, on some level, the mothering and fathering I was receiving was wrong. When I told my parents I was going to change things when I grew up I was laughed at and called naïve. My teenage years were rebellious ones. The anger I carried gave me a false sense of power. To show any other feelings felt too dangerous. The adult world was cruel and ridiculous to me. I lost interest in school. I had thoughts of suicide but not the courage to act on them. I spent little time at home and ignored curfews. It was on one of these nights after a serious argument that my mother told me about my biological mother. She told me she was a teenager and then half whispered "and only seventeen" and for my own protection she thought we should keep it a secret. I was also told that my biological mother had left a letter for me to read when I was old enough. Somehow this letter disappeared. I was devastated. My birth seemed nothing to be proud of. At fifteen I felt I did not belong anywhere. I was falling apart.

One afternoon my mother nervously asked me why I believed my father was so hard on me.

The dam burst and I revealed my secret in hope of finally being understood. Instead, I was asked to leave so my mother could confront him. I had no idea where to go or when or if I should return. I was homeless and stayed wherever I could. I had no money and rarely ate. I became very ill and was hospitalized. I was too terrified to go home and a girlfriend's mother took me in and cared for me. As a struggling single mother, it must have been a difficult decision to take on another child. I am grateful for her kindness and sacrifice. I did eventually go home. It was as if nothing had happened. I realized then that I could no longer live with these people.

At sixteen I met a man six years older. While we were dating, I confided in him all that had happened. He and his family helped me to leave permanently. I was exhausted, broken and needed a safe place to be taken care of. I accepted the help willingly. They were so kind to me over the next seven years. They will always have a special place in my heart. Our relationship was not meant to be permanent, however, and at twenty-three I left to venture out on my own.

I have been living in Halifax since I was nineteen. My father died shortly after I moved here. We never really spoke before he died. There was no apology, no confrontation, and no closure. I had to find my own way to understand all I had lived through and what it all meant for my future. I certainly understood my life would never be a conventional one. I had drifted away from my family. There would be no boyfriends taken home to meet the folks. Reminiscing with family was and still is awkward. We have very little in common. The reality of my life is too painful for my mother to discuss. I cannot pretend none of it happened. I am a painful reminder of all that was wrong. It took years for me to understand that even without the sexual abuse all would not have been well. It was a symptom of much deeper problems. I was determined not to follow the same path.

At a young age I knew in my heart that I would experience motherhood. I also felt it would somehow be one of my greatest achievements. Underneath all the negativity projected onto my being female, behind the anger I felt at the injustices, which dishonored the female spirit, at my core, I was in love with who I was meant to be. This was my own little secret; there was something truly special about being a female, but I had yet to understand what it meant. The depth of these feelings amazed me, for I had no idea of their source. To tap into this source has over the years been instrumental in transforming the negative self-image I have carried since birth. It is ongoing, both rewarding and painful.

My healing did not really begin until I gave birth to my son at the age of twenty-six. I wanted to mother my son differently. It was my son who showed me the way. Children are great teachers. Our relationship has been going on nearly twelve years. It has not always been easy. I believe our children are very patient with us adults. After all, they are closer to the source. I, however, have had to find my way back to that source.

I have learned over these past twelve years that I am a mother by definition. I gave birth; therefore I am a mother. It does not make me, or any mother, more or less of a woman. But it is not for everyone nor should it be. To be a mother or father is an act of biology. The art of mothering or fathering is not the same thing. It is a deep individual and personal process. We are not all the same. It is absolutely an art form and I am an artist. It is outside of society's rigid beliefs. A true artist will say that they are only bringing forth what is already there waiting to emerge. They are the vehicle to guide it into being. I honestly believe this is a profound truth. I dishonor a sacredness when I try to control or manipulate to suit my past beliefs or society's expectations. I move away from the source. This source can only be accessed through an open heart. This is the place of love. The source is love; it is where we all come from. It is not an easy place to get to and even more difficult to live in on a daily basis because it is free of judgement. Since we have all been weaned to judge or be judged it seems unattainable.

To me this is not about an end but about the process. I can never be totally free of all the negative influences, which keep me making mistakes. I will never be a saint and that is not my goal. I struggle often with all of this. When I veer off of my path through the stresses of living, I find I have to sit still for awhile. I have to focus on opening my heart up to free myself from the judgements I place on myself and others, as well as those directed towards me. The more I allow myself to do this the less time I spend off the path and stuck in the old patterns of shame, guilt and blame. I am no longer as attracted to these negative thoughts and feelings. What once felt like instinct now is choice. I am no longer like a moth to a flame. To change perceptions and move to a higher consciousness does not mean we will be mistake free, just as laws implemented to effect change cannot guarantee to open hearts. It can be a long process.

There are many ways to connect to this source of love. Artists come in many forms and we are all artists in our own way. We are true artists when what we do is an act of love. It is vital to remember this when interacting especially with children and not just our own. I have often heard adults talk about children whom they consider to be bad or out of control, but they have never talked to them. A so-called bad child is usually broken, hurting or neglected in some way. Talking about them accomplishes nothing. We are all responsible for channeling as much love as we can to all children. We do not necessarily have to give birth to be able to mother or father a child.

I should make it clear at this point that I in no way feel this process exclusive only to mothering. It is not gender based. We need to address this division of male and female in regard to children. The conditioning a lot of males receive keeps them far from this process and I find this disturbing. We tend to take for granted, therefore dishonoring, people when we do not take the time to truly understand how we have labeled and lumped them into stereotypical roles. We do not see how we oppress others with our words, our mannerisms, our rules and our indifference. Our distorted assumptions about others keep them down and tend to make us look good. But it is a short-lived feeling. We hold on to our rigid perceptions of winners and losers, good and bad, black and white, young and old, women and men, rich and poor, heaven and hell. There are those who work hard and those we think are lazy. We have those who are good parents and those who are not. The list goes on and on. We are quick to throw everyone into a category and we all hope to God we get thrown in amongst the good ones. The pressure to live up to everyone's perceptions is great. This hatred and discrimination will probably always be amongst and within us. We need to choose to transform this negative energy. For just a little change can have positive repercussions we may not immediately realize.

As we learn to honor mothering and fathering as an art form, we will see the outcome in our children. There will be less to mend, less shame, less hopelessness and despair. We will not accept living in utter poverty and the exploitation of others. We will all learn to hold each other up. We will educate the heart not just the mind. We will learn to inspire rather than instill. We will use less force and show more patience. In all, we will learn to acknowledge the artist in each of us.

I have come to understand that my birth was not a mistake. I came into this world with an open heart, but those around me had closed theirs. They became blind with pain and fear, so they could not see me for who I truly was. My needs were left unmet, just as I am sure theirs were. But the heart cannot be closed permanently — there is always a way back in. This is my journey. I came into the world open-hearted and this is the way I choose to leave it.

Candace Bernard

The journey to womanhood

My mother married my father in 1975, and I was born a year and a half later in 1976. At the time of my birth, both of my parents were hard working students. My father was attending the Nova Scotian College of Art and Design, while my mother worked on her Master of Social Work (MSW) degree at Dalhousie. My father drove a taxi at night while in school full time. My mother was pregnant with me while in graduate school. She gave birth to me during her Christmas break and returned to school in January, taking me to classes with her.

My father previously worked as a sleeping car porter, as this was one of the few types of employment available to African Nova Scotian men, other than janitorial or hard laboring jobs. He began the job at seventeen and worked there for seven years before deciding to return to school. My father did not want to retire working for VIA Rail, and was determined to start a new career. When he decided to return to school, my father was the first from his family and the first African Nova Scotian man from his community to attend university. He became one of the first formally educated African Nova Scotian artists, and the first African Nova Scotian professional photographer.

After graduating with her MSW, my mother worked as a psychiatric social worker, then as a family therapist, before taking a full-time teaching position at Dalhousie. Interestingly, I graduated with my MSW at the same age my mother was when she graduated with her MSW. During her time as a front line social worker, my mother experienced racism from her peers, supervisors and clients. This prompted her to become one of the four founding members of the Association of Black Social Workers in 1979. My parents were always involved in social action, as I recall attending various meetings and rallies with them in the community.

Both of my parents started legacies of higher education in their respective families, as well as the larger African Nova Scotian community. They have helped pave the way in higher education for the next generation, and I have always admired them for achieving these accomplishments in the face of adversity. My parents were determined to provide me with advantages that were unavailable to them and did their best to shelter me from many things, including a racist and sexist society. They were also determined to start new family traditions of their own, which included no physical discipline, and no gender divisions.

My mother remembers growing up in a household with five boys and seven girls. The girls did all of the domestic chores, including cooking and cleaning for their brothers. This work began at a young age, especially after my grandfather died. My grandmother had to work full time, and the girls in the family were expected to cook, clean, comb each other's hair, provide assistance with homework, and babysit. My parents attempted to provide a gender neutral environment by purchasing a range of toys and games for me. My household responsibilities included indoor and outdoor chores (which were often left to men or boy children). In addition, my parents wanted me to be assertive and did not believe that children should be seen and not heard.

Although I grew up in a White neighborhood and attended all White schools, my parents exposed me to my African Nova Scotian community. My parents instilled in me traditional African Nova Scotian values such as respect for elders and community involvement. In addition, I attended Brownies and Girl Guides in East Preston (an African Nova Scotian community), and attended an African Nova Scotian church where our family was actively involved. We maintained a strong connection to our extended family and the extended community. These experiences have fostered a strong community connection.

Traveling was an important part of my education. My parents made sacrifices to give me that experience. Travel experience gave me valuable learning opportunities and positive exposure to other African descended people. I was amazed when we traveled to places in the United States, where there is a significant population of African Americans. We visited African American universities and it was the first time in my life that I had seen such a strong presence of other African descended people in positions of power and authority. This experience was empowering and affirming. One thing that surprised me was that many African Americans and people from other countries were always shocked to find out we were from Canada. To African Americans, Canada is viewed as the cold White North.

What was most painful for me was going to Africa and seeing our brothers and sisters, and discovering that many of them were unaware that there are African descended people living in Canada. The opportunity to travel to Africa and touch the soil of my ancestral homeland was one that I will always treasure. Traveling to Africa was possible when we lived in England. We moved to Sheffield, England, when my mother returned to university to complete a PhD. I was nervous about moving to England, as I held some of the same assumptions about England as many African Americans have about Canada. However, I was pleasantly surprised to find that England has a significant population of African descended people.

Watching my mother return to school at age thirty-nine was a wonderful experience. She encouraged many people of all ages to return or stay in school. While in England, we also traveled throughout Europe, where we experienced extreme forms of racism. For instance, one Brazilian man who was part of our tour group was harassed, beaten and arrested in Switzerland for simply walking the streets. This was a harsh example of the racism that prevails throughout the West.

Living at the intersection of race, class and gender

Knowing that they could not protect me from a racist and sexist environment, my parents tried to equip me with analytical tools, so that I might understand how racism and sexism will impact on my life and how to fight back. I remember clearly my first experience with racism.

It happened in my neighborhood school, which was an all White community. I was called nigger and other derogatory names by some of the students in the school and was constantly harassed about the color of my skin. Those experiences were very overt forms of racism; however, there were more subtle forms as well. For instance, a teacher and the principal at the school were intent on holding me back a grade, despite the fact that I was working at grade level. The school authorities used the fact that I withdrew socially (which was a result of the racism) as a rationale for the decision. These memories stand out very clearly in my mind because it was the first time I learned that being an African Nova Scotian was used as a basis for name calling and differential treatment. I also remember that the teachers, the principal and everybody in the school system refused to do anything about it. Action was taken only when my parents decided to do something about it.

In the process of doing this reflection, I discovered that my parents took the case to the Human Rights Commission and won. After we won the human rights case against the school board, and finally received an apology, my parents refused to put me back into the same system that created these problems, as no immediate structural change had occurred. They were able to use their economic resources to place me back into a private school where I began my formal education. My parents were forced to use this recourse as every accessible authority in the public system failed to acknowledge and address the racism I experienced. That was an awful experience, which could have been more detrimental if my parents did not have the ability and the resilience to fight the system and the resources to put me in a different environment.

It was in the private system where I discovered class differences. Paying for an education meant that the school authorities could not ignore you. When I faced racism in this environment (for example hearing racist jokes, comments, etc.), it was dealt with promptly and appropriately. The racism was also much more subtle.

I attended this school during the Cole Harbour High School race riots in 1989. My parents were very vocal and active in speaking out against this incident. The three of us were featured on the local evening news and on a national televison news program, as the media thought that our story was fascinating. That is, the fact that our family lived practically across the street from Cole Harbour High, yet my parents sent me to private school several years ago, when they had predicted something like this would happen. I recall walking into school shortly after the riots occurred and hearing a racist joke in the hallway. One young man said to another, "Where's the one place where you see a Black man in a suit? . . . In court!" I was horrified and the young men were unaware that I was within earshot. This joke was told after the fact that more African Nova Scotian male students than their White counterparts were arrested after the riots.

I discovered years later that my mother requested culturally appropriate materials for the private school library. However, during my years at the school I never knew these materials were available, as I was never presented with an opportunity to access them. Thus inclusiveness in schooling must occur on many levels to have a significant impact on student experiences. For instance, I had my first Black teacher while attending this school which was an affirming experience. However, the curriculum and overall ethnocentric attitude underpinning the school culture needed to be challenged.

The varying societal class levels and how they operated became clear to me at private school. For instance, class was the primary reason why, at many times, I was the only African Nova Scotian or person of African descent attending the P-12 school. I was completely surrounded by people who valued individualism, capitalism and competition. These values were in direct contrast to the African Nova Scotian values that my parents attempted to give me which include: collective responsibility (giving back to community), non materialism (valuing non material qualities in people such as honesty and integrity) and cooperation (working collaboratively with others). I often felt as though I was living in two very different worlds.

This reality made the experience extremely isolating. Therefore, I decided to request a return to the public system to complete high school. I felt in order for me to survive socially I had to go into an environment where I would have access to more students of color who were my age. Although the education at the private school was superior to that offered in the public system, I felt that it was more important for me at the time to be able to attend school with other African Nova Scotians. My parents respected and supported my choice and encouraged me to take action against the racism they knew I would face in the public school system. As a compromise, I attended Dartmouth High School, as opposed to Cole Harbour High School.

The stereotypes and the racism that I experienced as an individual at private school (i.e. as the only African Nova Scotian student in the school) differed from the experiences that the African Nova Scotian students in the public school faced as a group. The majority of African

Nova Scotian students traveled together in groups. The fact that we were African Nova Scotian, traveled in a group, and represented a completely different ethos from the norm made us quite a visible minority. (I use the term minority here only to reflect that as a student group, African Nova Scotian students made up a small percentage of the overall student body. I do not use the term minority to refer to African Nova Scotians as a racial group. From a global perspective, African and African descended people are not a minority population.) The peer group structure provided a safe place for us African Nova Scotian students to be ourselves without being stereotyped, ridiculed, or facing ignorance from those unfamiliar with the culture.

Stereotypes would come from everyone in the system, but it is particularly frustrating when you are stereotyped by a teacher, as it can put a strain on teacher–student relationships and classroom interaction. I remember a teacher whom the majority of African Nova Scotian students had major problems with. We tried to get to the root of what the problems were and arranged a private meeting. He admitted to my mother and me that his fears were rooted in the fact that he was robbed by a Black man several years ago. He was obviously afraid of Black people, particularly the Black people who dressed or acted in non-conformist, non middle-class ways. Those were the students who had the most difficult time with him.

When I am stereotyped as an African Nova Scotian female, I am grouped into race, class and gender specific stereotypes. My gender experiences are directly linked to my race. In terms of class it was no coincidence that the majority of the Black students at the public school were coming from lower social economic backgrounds, and there is also no coincidence that I was one of less than seven Black students who attended the private school over a ten year span. My own experiences compelled me to do research in this area. My MA thesis focuses on how race, class and gender influence the educational experiences of African Nova Scotian students. As a social worker, I examine how individuals fit within a matrix of oppression, as opposed to only examining how one particular form of oppression shapes the lives of my clients.

Doing social action

While I attended public school, my parents were involved in school activities and my mother would occasionally drop by the school. This made the teachers and principal very nervous. They did not know how to treat my mother as she did not fit into one of their stereotypical images of Black mothers. She was an educated, married, professional woman, the opposite of what they expected her to be. They felt they had no choice but to respect and listen to her (something they had not done with parents of other African Nova Scotian children), as they were afraid of the recourse she would take. For example, my mother planned to accompany me to one particular class because of the racism I and several others were experiencing from the teacher. With only the suggestion being made, she never had to act on it.

I quickly learned that the public system had not changed since my departure ten years prior. There were still expectations that African Nova Scotian students would not succeed, at least not to the same degree as their white counterparts. I spent a significant amount of time in high school challenging the types of things that were going on. I challenged teachers who I thought were racist. Examples of the types of action taken include the following: our peer group started chapters of both the Cultural Awareness Youth Group and the Parents of Black Children; I arranged for my mother to facilitate cultural sensitivity training for teachers and staff; when we discovered the school had not done anything for African Heritage Month, we took around the video *Speak It!* to show people during different classes; we lobbied to remove "classic" literature that we thought was racist from the curriculum. Some of those books have since been removed. I also arranged for myself and other African Nova Scotian students to study African American and African Canadian literature, instead of some of the racist material that we were expected to read. My interest in African literature flourished after that.

I remember occasionally wearing Africentric clothing to school. I started my own Africentric clothing company so I could have access to those clothes because many stores would not sell them. It was very important to be able to identify with various forms of culture that related to our experiences. Books, movies, clothing were very important and facilitated positive esteem and racial pride. Unfortunately, social action had to be taken in order to make space within the system for cultural expression. The social action activities I engaged in were very rewarding, and taught me useful skills such as organization, effective means of protest, non-violent confrontation, and assertiveness. These skills are important to have when dealing with racism and other forms of oppression on a daily basis. Nevertheless, the school is an environment that should be providing supports for, and making space for, the entire student body.

Reflections on the journey of learning

I never viewed finishing high school as a major accomplishment, because I was taught at a very a young age that if you do not have your education then you are going to have a very hard time in life, as an African Nova Scotian woman. Therefore, I saw graduating from high school as a stepping-stone, something I had to do to get to where I was going. In retrospect, however, it was an accomplishment because too many African Nova Scotian students have not survived the system. Black parents must prepare their children for the realities of racism, sexism, classism and other forms of oppression. This method of parenting has been described as the "politics of Black Motherhood" (Bernard & Bernard, 1998; P.H. Collins, 1990; Scott, 1991). It can be described as "a necessary dualism [that Black mothers face] preparing their daughters for a life of other-imposed disempowerment and the vision and courage to resist and overcome such oppression" (Bernard & Bernard, 1998, p. 47).

As an African Nova Scotian graduate student I felt even more isolated than I did at high school. As I moved further into higher education, I saw the number of people who look like me decrease significantly. For instance, as a graduate student, I saw a significant decrease in the number of graduate students of African descent in comparison to the number of African undergraduate students. I saw even fewer numbers of African students engaged in post graduate study. Furthermore, there are even fewer professors. For instance, it was important for me to have an African descended person on my MA thesis committee; however, in order to do this, I had to look in the community. I could not find a local professor of African descent, in my field of study within the academy, who could meet my needs. My story is not an isolated case. I have talked to African graduate students studying across the country who face similar dilemmas. I see this as a serious gap, which has prompted me to consider doing a PhD, so that I can be a mentor for others.

My reason for wanting to be a social worker is rooted in my own experience, and my wish to make a difference in the African Nova Scotian community. There are many inequities that exist for African Nova Scotians. Even though there have been some great initiatives, many disparities remain. African Nova Scotians are still not entering university and post secondary education at the same rate as our White counterparts. We are still over represented in the number of people on income assistance, and the number of people living on and below the poverty line. We are still earning less money, still underemployed, and still unemployed to an alarming degree. I often ask myself, "Why?" The African Nova Scotian community has realized since their arrival in Nova Scotia that education is what will make the community upwardly mobile. We need to critically examine the things that will continue to make the community stronger. We need to continue to look at the blocks and barriers that we face in trying to move forward. As a social worker, I have attempted to work toward the goal of equality for all African Nova Scotians and other oppressed people.

Conclusion

To conclude, I must say that this journey to womanhood is ongoing. There have been many challenges along the way. Although painful, in retrospect, these have been growth enhancing experiences. As a young African Nova Scotian woman, I have not had the benefit of being directly involved in critical movements for social change, such as the women's movement or civil rights movements. However, my experiences as the child of community activists and my own personal journey into womanhood have been good training ground for a future in social justice and social change.

For further reading

Bernard, W., Bernard, C. (1998). "Passing the Torch: A Mother and Daughter Reflect on their Experiences Across Generations." *Canadian Women's Studies,* 18 (2,3), 46-51.

Collins, Patricia H. (1990). *Black Feminist Thought: Knowledge, Consciousness and the Politics of Empowerment.* New York: Routledge

Scott, Kesho Y. (1991) *The Habit of Surviving.* New York. Ballantrail Books

Leah M.F. Caitlin

private practice psychotherapist

"Don't play with men or you'll get hurt."

"Marriage, you don't know the *half* of it."

"Make sure you can always support yourself."

"That's the way things are, that's the way they've always been and that's the way they'll stay."

"Such is this life, nothing we can do." (The inevitability of it all.)

"What will the neighbours say . . . "

Such were the words of wisdom told to me by the elder women in my family. Words to believe or words to rebel against? I probably did both.

I married young, but didn't find out what my grandmother's other "half" was. I went to university, twice, to train for professions that would support me. I found out that women as well as men can hurt you, and I no longer worry about what the neighbours will think.

I am still rebelling against the notion that things cannot change. It is not by chance that my work as a psychotherapist is all about change.

As a young girl, I knew about the injustices my mother experienced in her work as a personal secretary to two development tycoons. She had one of the most responsible jobs in their establishment, but she was *automatically* paid less than any man in any position in the firm. When I asked her why, she said that men were paid more because they were the heads of households and were raising families and that most women worked for "pin money." (This was the 1950s.)

I knew that my mother, as a single parent, was not working for "pin money"; she was working so that we could eat and pay the rent. My mother took the attitude that since she hadn't been able to "keep" her marriage together, thereby ensuring that my father would be there to support us, then she just had to take what she could get in the way of wages. She had no benefits, no sick pay, no overtime (although she frequently worked more than forty hours a week) and she had no power. She was not in a position to fight for more money because doing so might mean that she could lose her job. I do not think she was angry. "That's just the way things are," she would say. And in my little 10-year-old mind I thought, "Well, they don't have to be." Of course, I had no idea how things might or could change and soon I would experience injustices, based on gender, myself.

For instance in grade nine I wanted to take drafting. This was considered to be a "boys" course, as home economics was a "girls" course. I attempted to register anyway. The shop teacher told me that I could not take the course because I was a girl. Inside, I thought, "I didn't know that you needed a penis to do drafting, I thought you just needed a pencil!" In those days, nice young ladies did not talk that way to teachers. I went to the Principal to state my case. He said he would think about it. Later he came back with the solution . . . if I could find fourteen other girls who wanted to take drafting, he would set up an extra class. I asked why I could not just go into the regular class. He replied, "I can't have one girl, and a very pretty one at that, in a class

156

of thirty-five boys . . . they'll be too distracted to do their work." What about them distracting me?

My awareness of personal injustice continued. At sixteen I was looking forward to getting a summer job with The Blackball Ferry Company that traveled the BC coast to Alaska. My boyfriend had had a job with this company since he was sixteen. The hiring office secretary said the company didn't hire girls under the age of twenty-one. When I asked, "Why?" she said it was Company Policy. I asked to speak to her manager. He explained that they just couldn't be "responsible" for girls under twenty-one. I mentioned they had boys under that age on their ships and his reply was, "Well, my dear, to be perfectly blunt, boys don't get pregnant." Inside, I thought, "Well, my dear, the girls don't get pregnant by themselves, do they?" A Baby Feminist was being born.

A few years later I was confronted with the discriminatory policies of the Housing Residences at the University of British Columbia. There were Men's buildings and Women's buildings. The residents of the Women's buildings had an 11 p.m. curfew. The men had no restrictions. The housing office employee told me that since "girls" came from all over British Columbia (there were only two universities in the province at the time) the university felt that they had to act like parents and "protect" the girls sent to their care. I guess they were protecting us from the unrestricted men.

I was able to get through university without much harm and got my first teaching job in 1964. This was the only profession that I knew of that paid men and women equally and this was one of the reasons I chose it. I also loved working with children and was good at it. In the middle of September, I discovered that I was pregnant. The Vancouver School District policy was that no teacher could be four months pregnant and still be in the classroom.

I was then two months pregnant and I was in my probationary year. In BC one has to teach for one year before being issued a Permanent Teaching Certificate. So, like my mother, I didn't protest. I put in my resignation. I didn't question, I didn't fight. I didn't want to jeopardize my chance of being able to teach the following year. Now I was in my mother's shoes.

Fortunately, for me, the Women's Movement was beginning. By the end of the 1960s women's consciousness raising groups were forming and my community had a "Women's Centre" (full of lesbians, said all the husbands). Betty Friedan had published *The Feminist Mystique*; Gloria Steinem and Germaine Greer were writing about the very concerns that had affected me. I saw new hope for my daughter's future. Happily, I was accused of being one of those "libbers." We tried to make a lot of trouble wherever we went. It didn't take much.

After my second child was born, my husband and I moved to the United States so that he could take a degree in an alternative healing profession. Six months later, I followed him into this school because I thought I might just end up being his office "girl" if I didn't. This was not the most noble reason to go into a profession, but I ended up enjoying the education and the subsequent work. I agreed with the concept of medical care encompassing mind, body and spirit. Holistic health care offered an alternative way for people to become well. This profession suited my desire to be involved with something that went against the idea of "this is the way it is" (which conventional medicine represented to me at the time).

After practicing in New England, we came back to Canada. People have asked me, "Why did you come to Nova Scotia?" We had come home via Montreal and since we had seen all of the Transcanada Highway from Victoria to Montreal, we thought we would take the opportunity to visit the Maritimes before we headed west. Well, you know what Halifax looks like on an autumn day — magnificent foliage, sunny skies, no rain. So, like many others, we stayed.

I do not recall any gender related discrimination in my education or professional life, but the rest of the world was still full of it. Luckily, in my office building in Bedford, I discovered an organization called Supportive Action for Women. I went up to find out what they were all about and met the director, Marie Armstrong. She told me that the organization worked with women who were starting out or returning to the work force. They did vocational counselling, assertiveness training and had job finding clubs. Soon I was doing workshops for this group, became a board member and eventually chairperson of the board. One of the women on the board, Diane Swinimar, later became the director of the Metro Food Bank (a job she still holds). Most of the board members were from Sackville and Bedford. Although we might not all have identified ourselves as "feminists," our work was for the benefit of women.

In my professional life, I was becoming more interested in the role of stress as it related to illness and therefore continued my training in psychotherapy. In the 1980s many women in North America and Europe had benefited from the battles of feminists before them and were now able to seemingly have it "all" (marriage, children and a career). "The Superwoman Syndrome" was driving many women into chronic fatigue, depression and anxiety. And I found much of my work was related to women's stress, not men's. This is still true today, and 80 percent of my clients are female.

A significant part of the Women's Movement in Nova Scotia was made manifest by the production of the newspaper *Pandora*. Originally conceived by Betty Ann Lloyd and later produced by a women's collective, this newspaper gave a voice to women, and only to women. We refused to accept articles from men. And so, a few years later, a man protested to the Human Rights Commission. There was a tribunal and I testified, among others, about the need for a woman only forum. *Pandora* won the case and was published for a few more years. During this same time the Women's Health Education Network (WHEN) began. For more than ten years, we held an annual two-day conference. Women from all around the province gave and attended workshops and activities related to women's health. I found that belonging to these organizations provided me with the possibility of making change. I was no longer in my mother's shoes; I now had shoes all around me filled by women who also wanted change.

In the mid 1980s, I was into personal change as well. The focus of my practice changed from the physical to the emotional, my personal style became more assertive, I continued my education and I left my marriage. A long period of emotional chaos ensued. I moved my office from Bedford to Halifax and began living in a flat owned by the Halifax Women's Housing Cooperative.

Two events were soon to happen to me that would change my life forever . . . I would travel to Peru and I would once again be in my mother's shoes . . . diagnosed with the same illness that had killed her.

Witnessing suffering and extreme poverty, combined with terrorist and military violence in Peru made me acutely aware of my First World privileges. Despite the problems of hunger, illness and physical danger surrounding them, the women at the Lima Feminist Centre educated and protested for the rights of women. Communities of religious women organized cooperative schools, cooperative craft businesses, health centres, communal soup kitchens, libraries, and shelters for abused women and for women who were in the sex trade. I returned from South America much more aware of the need to fight for human rights and much more aware of the suffering of others. I also came away inspired by optimism and buoyed by the bravery of those I had met.

Once back in Nova Scotia I joined a political party; marched for human rights, specifically sexual orientation rights; attended Hiroshima Day Memorials; walked in Take Back the Night marches; supported the National Action Committee and considered myself politically active. This was an overstatement, considering that I was in the same community as Muriel Duckworth (Order of Canada) and Betty Peterson (peace activist).

The impact of the symptoms of systemic lupus erythematosus brought me face to face with my own mortality. In my forties, I was asking myself . . . will I live another five years or ten? . . . what should I do with my life now? . . . what is the purpose of life? . . . what do I want to do in the future, especially if I have only a short future? . . . how am I going to earn my living? Unconsciously, I mimicked my mother's reaction to her illness . . . just keep going, act as if you feel fine when you don't and never complain. Mom's message, were she still alive, would have been "Don't feel sorry for yourself." I am not sure if my stoical behavior actually worsened my condition.

During the last twelve years, I have been forced, by my illness to slow down at work and home — to become less involved in community action and to take more time to smell the roses. This has been a period of spiritual growth for me. I am more certain of my values, more certain of what I believe and more certain of what I want to do with my life.

I believe in human rights.

I believe that humans can learn and change.

I believe that the fight for justice is always worthwhile.

I believe that the communal effort of many can change institutions and societies.

I believe that love is essential.

So unlike the words left to me, I hope that these beliefs are the ones my children remember and live by.

As for myself, I am now comforted and inspired by the following:

> To laugh often and much; to win the respect of intelligent people and the affection of children; to earn the appreciation of honest critics and endure the betrayal of false friends; to appreciate beauty; to find the best in others; to leave the world a bit better, whether by a healthy child, a garden patch, or a redeemed social condition; to know even one life has breathed easier because you have lived. This is to have succeeded. — Ralph Waldo Emerson

Patti Doyle-Bedwell

Director, Transition Year Program, Dalhousie University
Director, Program for Indigenous Blacks & Mi'kmaq,
Dalhousie Law School

I dedicate my story to the memory of Joshua Loren Frank Doyle.
I love you and miss you terribly.

May 23, 2000 — The talking circle is an Aboriginal ceremony, which allows people to speak freely. In this story, I am taking the talking stick and telling you who I am as a Mi'kmaq woman.

I am sitting in Yellowknife, NWT. I am on the Governor General's Canadian Study tour. Earlier, we met with representatives of women's groups and the Salvation Army. They began describing their typical client. Sexually abused, drug addicted, poor, female, single parent, Aboriginal.

I felt the familiar pain of my own experience. I tried very hard to hide it during the presentation. My tour group consisted of many suc-

162

cessful people, some who sat in shock at this description of the Salvation Army's typical client. At the end of the day, the group discussed the situation and the tragedies and hopelessness of Aboriginal people. I facilitated the group that night and when I had the chance to share, I said, "Welcome to my world." And I started to cry. I began to look back on my life and knew that nothing is ever hopeless. I finally got it; I have been given many gifts, most importantly, one of healing.

My father and mother never thought they would have a child. Thirty-five years old, Mom felt that she would never have children. Then I came along, on November 11, 1958. She had a difficult birthing experience but undaunted, she got pregnant again and had my sister on September 21, 1960. My father was Irish; he was born in 1900, in Rochester, New York. He tried to be a writer, but I do not know if he ever published anything. However, he wrote a song for me, which a local Maine band recorded when I was born; my mother still has the record.

I grew up in Bangor, Maine, went to Catholic schools from kindergarten to grade twelve. In the summers, we travelled to my mother's home reserve in Cape Breton. I grew up immersed in the Mi'kmaq culture, but I did not realize it at the time. I didn't realize it until I was in law school. But more on that later.

My father died when I was seven years old. He had a heart attack on a Sunday morning, on December 12, 1965. I felt that my life changed quite radically from that point on. I miss my father and I think of him often. I had a difficult time grieving his death. I don't think that I really grieved until I was very much older. I remember feeling scared. For many years, I didn't remember what happened after he died, I blocked it out of my mind. I remember my father telling me to be proud that I am Irish as well as Mi'kmaq. I remember my father having tremendous respect for John F. Kennedy, because he was the first Irish Catholic president. I remember JFK's pictures in our house. My father wrote President Kennedy a letter and my mother still has the letter and the response.

I did not go to my father's funeral; I was very scared of the word "died." I remember touching my father at the wake and he was very cold. I did not understand what was happening.

I became very ill after my father died, I remember being in the hospital with ulcerative colitis. I also remember that many doctors came to see me because normally children did not get this disease. I lost a lot of weight and had a very restricted diet. For five years, I suffered from this disease and all its complications, such as anemia and arthritis. I could not do sports; I sometimes could not walk. I know that my disease placed a great burden on my mother, both emotionally and financially. She worked at the hospital as a dietary aid and kitchen worker. The hospital deducted my medical expenses from her check, a little each week.

After my father died, we did not move back to the reserve despite my mom's relatives arguing with her about it. When my mom married my dad, she lost her Indian status. Our reserve told her she could move back if she would say she never married my dad. She would not do that. My mother also worked as a domestic. I remember going with her to a very big house, which belonged to a doctor, sitting on the little bench and not being allowed to touch anything. I always felt good about our life. I was amazed that people lived in big houses and had lots of stuff, which we could not touch. I could not imagine living a life where there was enough of everything.

When I was little, I loved to read. Words created magic in my life; I could see the action in my mind, I could visualize the characters, and the locations. I dreamed of travelling to faraway places. Reading helped me to escape. I remember my father reading to me when I was small. I have also kept a journal since I was in fourth grade. I wrote what I considered poetry. I could always pour out my feelings on the blank page. I loved school and I always did very well. My mom used to get mad at me for reading late into the night, with a flashlight, under the covers. I loved mysteries and I loved biographies. I always loved people stories and I would read everything I could get my hands on. I wrote in my journal and I still have some of them from when I was younger.

My mother always talked about the importance of an education. She always said that we needed to be independent, and not to depend upon a man to support us. I think that was borne out of her experience of being a widow at a young age. She had little or no marketable skills. She always pushed us to do well in school. She wanted us to go to university. But I always had difficulty believing that I had any brains at all. When I was in fourth grade, I received all As in my courses. I went to the teacher and asked her if I really deserved those grades as I thought my teacher had made a mistake. She assured me that I really did deserve those marks. That teacher also picked me out of the class all the time and introduced me to visitors as "the smartest girl in the class who is one half Irish and one half Indian, can you believe it?" I never knew what part was more unbelievable. I did not know that being Indian was a bad thing.

I could also read very fast as a child. I remember being tested and being in the 99 percentile. My reading speed was 1,200 words a minute in grade five. The school placed me in reading classes which were always three or four grades ahead of my current grade. I always wanted to read books far ahead of my grade level, which upset the teachers to no end.

I also wanted to help people. I remember being so sad at seeing poor people on the street. We never had much money after my father died. Some things seemed forever out of reach, like new clothes. I remember my mother searching the house for a quarter to buy bread or a dime to buy a small container of milk. I remember travelling to Cape Breton when family members became ill and getting in trouble at school because I missed a lot of time. I remember Christmas days when we did not get many presents.

I believed, as a young child, in justice and fairness. To me, it was simple: people needed to eat, they needed a place to live and society should take care of those who could not take care of themselves. When I was twelve, I wanted to build a big house for the poor people and give them a place to live and to prepare a hot meal. I wanted to take care of everyone who had less than I did. I wanted to change society. I wanted a society where poor people would not be poor any longer. I knew, from my own experience, how quickly life could change. My father died suddenly, without warning, and our lives changed so drastically from that moment.

I loved sports when I was a kid. I competed on a swim team after I recovered from colitis and I wanted to be the best. I travelled throughout the state of Maine and spent my summers swimming and running. My sister talked about our swimming period and we decided that sports saved us as we went though adolescence. The endorphins flying through our bodies kept us sane. I loved to travel to swim meets. I always had great fun. My mom drove us everywhere. She was also working at the hospital and she worked around our schedule.

In grade eight, Sister Helen arrived on the scene. She did not like me but I kept doing well in her classes, much to her chagrin. She got mad at me once when I was the last person, in the line-up, to pass in a history exam. She screamed at me that I was a stupid Indian and could not remember anything important. She ripped up my exam in front of the entire class. I remember I cried all day; my mother got very angry at the teacher. She went over right away and told the nun off for treating me so badly. I learned that teachers did not always have the right answers.

I went to high school at John Bapst High, a private Catholic high school. Everything was college prep. I sang in the glee club. I love to sing, even today, although I don't have a good voice (in other words, I am not as good as Sarah Maclaughlin). I measure myself against very high standards. I studied piano for about five years. I had a music teacher who told me that I didn't have the talent to study music beyond high school. I didn't care really because all I wanted to be able to do is play piano, which I can do. I also wanted to take dance but people told me that I was too tall. I finally took a dance class when I was thirty-seven. I still take jazz dance and I always feel like the hippo in *Fantasia* but I love to dance.

I felt very awkward since I was so tall. By fourteen, I stood at my full height of five feet nine inches. I was slim and tall and the boys in my class were short! Needless to say, I did not have many boyfriends. I did very well in high school and I made the honour roll many times. I also became a member of the National Honour Society for my GPA and my activities. During the summer between my junior year and senior year, the Maine High School Juniors Honours Program accepted me into University of Maine at Orono to take two credit courses.

During my teenage years, my sister got pregnant. I was in Boston and I remember coming home at Christmas. I so hoped she would have the baby before I went back to school. I thought my mother would be so upset when she found out about the pregnancy but as soon as my sister told her she was pregnant, Mom started planning the nursery. Josh came before I went to school. I had the honour of being there when Josh was born. I picked his middle name. I peeked through the door, and I saw his cute little head. I had never seen such a beautiful baby. I felt like his mother too. I felt such love for him. When Angel brought him home, we stayed awake, waiting for him to wake up. I remember giving him a bath in the kitchen, the room so warm and cosy.

Josh has always been a bright point in my life. My love for him helped me to survive the many trials and tribulations in my life. Josh and I always had such a blast. He was so funny when he was little. He was a very active little boy, and very smart. We used to jump in mud puddles together and play ball outside. I bought him toys and clothes. Sometimes he would stay with me in Halifax. He always felt bad that we didn't have a car. When we went to Cape Breton, I always took Josh with me to movies or out on the lake fishing. He was very scared of fishing when he was little, because of the worms. We canoed together, and we spent a lot of time together. I felt so much love for this little person. Really, the love I have in my heart for him was the first time I felt so fiercely protective of anyone.

Yet during this time, I felt completely unlovable, stupid, and I had many problems to deal with. During this time, before I made the move to Halifax, I made a half-hearted effort to commit suicide, I felt so despondent. I felt that I had no choices in my life and that I really was getting old fast (I was twenty years old!). I experienced drug and alcohol problems. I felt that if I married my "prince charming," my life would suddenly transform into one of purpose, love and togetherness. Growing up, I wanted so badly for someone to love me. In all my relationships, I tended to ignore the many negative signs that pointed out that perhaps this person was not the best guy for me, like serious alcohol and drug problems. In many of my relationships, I tried so hard to change the guy into someone better. Despite all the negativity, I persevered, in the hopes of changing him for the better, to be the man I wanted him to be. I did this over and over again.

During many relationships, I suffered from abuse. One incident occurred in the winter. I got hurt quite badly and I was so scared, I slept on the couch, in my high-rise apartment. I remember the snow falling outside, silently in the early dawn. I did not have a telephone so I went downstairs to call the police. I talked to the Halifax police and they would not come to the apartment. I remember the police officer telling me that it would be my word against his and nothing could be done.

I hung up the telephone and felt so defeated. I went back upstairs. I was so scared, I lay on my maroon love seat and tried to sleep, with a knife under my pillow for protection. I remember my hand throbbing with pain, and the pain was shooting up my arm. I decided once morning came, I should go to the hospital. The Halifax Infirmary was just down the street from my house. I walked there, in the snow. Because it was early and a Sunday, no cars passed me on the road. The snow came down in my eyes and it took me a long time to get to the hospital.

When I got there, the nurse asked me what was wrong with me. I did not dare tell her because of the reaction from the cops. I said that I fell down and hurt my hand. I went into x-ray. The doctor said my bones were shattered in my hand. He did not believe I had fallen; he said it looked like someone had taken a hammer to my hand. He set it and asked me whom he should call, as I was dopey from the medicine they had given me to set my hand. I told him to call my friend who turned around and called my partner. So he showed up to pick me up.

168

Apparently, he had no memory of kicking me. I did what I felt was the right thing; I went home with him.

I attended Dalhousie University during this time and decided to withdraw. I felt seriously depressed; I took many pain pills for my hand. I did not know how to get out of this relationship. I felt strongly that I had to do something but I could not find the energy to make a decision.

Suddenly, the fear left me. I did not feel scared anymore. I put my foot down and knew that I would never go back to him. Up to that point, I actually thought I could make the relationship work by twisting myself into a pretzel, but my anger saved me. The anger finally overtook the fear of being alone, of being unloved, since I finally got it, that love does not include violence. I was better off being alone than being afraid. I had a tremendous amount of support from my friends that helped me leave him for good.

I continued to work. However, I felt bored with my job. I felt the doors closing there. By 1990, I had a baby, I was a single parent, and I felt quite confident in my ability to parent, because I had taken care of Josh. Josh taught me to feel okay about taking care of Michael, but Josh did not like the fact that he was no longer the only grandchild. I remember that Josh and Mike did not get along until they got older. My time became very full of caring for Michael and working, trying to be a successful single mom.

During this time, I was also in therapy. I did not know what to do with my life. I was going to turn thirty and again felt so old. I sat home one day and did a questionnaire, which asked, "If you could do anything you wanted, with no barriers or worries, what would you do?" I wrote, "Go to law school." When I wrote that, I laughed out loud. No Mi'kmaq woman had gone to law school. I hadn't even finished my degree yet! But the dream percolated in my heart. I returned to school in 1989 for my honours in sociology.

I faced many of my fears about my abilities. I had to write a thesis, take all required courses and maintain a B average. I cried many times and I probably quit everyday. I just never had the energy to go through the process. I would tell myself, "One more day, see what happens tomorrow, read one more chapter, write one more paper, see how you do." I took school one day at a time.

I had two wonderful professors in sociology encourage me to think about applying to law school. I was quite shocked. I didn't tell anyone that I wanted to attend law. I still held on to my dream of helping people, helping women who had been abused. That experience drove me to apply, but I felt that I would not get in. I took it one step at a time; write the LSAT, see how you do, Patti, send in the application, bit by bit, face the fear.

June 1990 was a pivotal month. I finished my honours year, I found out I had diabetes and I finally told George I loved him with all my heart and soul. He is definitely my soul mate in life. Then, a bigger surprise. Dalhousie Law School accepted me! When I got the letter, I read it, dropped it on the floor and burst into tears. I really wanted Dalhousie to reject me. I could not believe I could really be a lawyer. I knew I would be a different lawyer. I believed that law would help me pursue justice. I got very scared. Carleton University had already accepted me in an MSW program but law was my dream. My friend Harris told me, "You are afraid you will fail law school. It is a much bigger risk than social work. Face your fear and do it!"

I struggled with law, not academically but culturally. I would run home to George and cry. I knew I was different. I turned to Trisha Monture who gave me the strength to continue my studies. I met wonderful people, friends who are still best friends today. Yet I felt so alienated there. So afraid! However, I knew that I was on the right path. I had no idea why, but knew that I had to chase my dreams and face my fear.

George and I are still together despite poverty, pain, grief and struggle. He is my best friend, my safe place. I am not afraid with him, he would never hurt me and I love him with all my heart and soul. He is a wonderful father to my son. I never would have graduated from law school without his love and support. We got married in June 1992.

My proudest moment occurred on that day in May when I graduated from law school. When I received my degree, I walked off the stage and my son, who was five years old, ran down the aisle at the Rebecca Cohn Auditorium and screamed, *"I love you, Mom!"* My entire family was there, all my nieces and nephews. It was the proudest moment of my life.

Despite my success, fear has been my constant companion. I have felt like a fraud. Yet I have moments of connection. I believe in God, I believe in love and that sometimes overcomes the fear. I never imagined I would be doing what I love, that I would travel, be on TV, and be invited to do public speaking engagements. I live my vision as much as possible. I still want to make this world a better place. I don't want my life to be wasted. I don't want to believe that I am worthless anymore but I still struggle with those feelings.

Inside, I am still the little Mi'kmaq–Irish girl who dreams of being a writer and a teacher, who misses her daddy, who still stares at and looks for pictures in clouds. Who still sings in the car, loves U2, the Police, Robbie Robertson, The Backstreet Boys, Mi'kmaq chanting, dolls, dance, and disco music. I love to read. I love books and can spend all day at Chapters and I read everything, including cereal boxes when nothing else is available. I love the ocean. I can sit and watch waves all day. My idea of fun is to sit on a beach with a good book. I love the mountains, tall, strong, and grounded. I love my son, my husband, and my family.

My son is the miracle in my life. The doctors never believed that I would carry him to term. However, on October 12, 1986, he came into the world, healthy and happy. I always tell Mike he is my miracle baby. I treasure the experience of his birth and his presence in my life. After three miscarriages, I am not able to have any more children. My children in the spirit world are special to me. Mike is here and I am so grateful. I also love my nieces and nephews and godchildren and all the "adopted" children we have, like David, who is Mike's best friend and who calls me Mom.

But the restlessness is beginning again. My life is beginning to move in a different direction. For instance, I have been the chair of the Nova Scotia Advisory Council on the Status of Women. I had the opportunity to travel, to give voice to my hopes, dreams and aspirations for women's equality. I have been in the public eye, speaking out on women's issues. The issues closest to my heart have been violence against women and education. Working for the Council has been a warm, wonderful and empowering experience.

When I was on the Governor General Study Tour, I met such wonderful people in my group. Before I left for Banff, I knew my tour group members would be my teachers. I was so afraid of being judged. However, my tour group members taught me to face my fear, to speak my mind, to share my joy and pain. I went down into an icehouse in Tuktoyaktuk petrified out of my mind. I stood looking into that dark hole, the slippery icy wooden ladder and I could not see to the bottom. Jim and Joe helped me go down that dark hole. I shook all the way down. I saw the permafrost. I have a picture of me down in the icehouse. I know I can face my fear. I came back believing I can do anything. My tour group members changed me. I know they will stay in my heart and soul and their caring will sustain me, forever.

I look back at my life and realize that God has blessed me so much. I have travelled across this country many times. I have been to Europe to the United Nations. I have spoken from my heart and from my experience.

I do not know the direction my life will take, but I know that changes are on the horizon. I know that I can't change other people's racism against me or their sexism. I do not believe their lies anymore. I have begun to jettison those negative beliefs. I have learned to take risks and speak my mind. I have learned to let go, just a bit.

In the North, the land spoke to me. I felt spiritually connected to that land, to the Arctic Ocean and the mountains. I will never forget that feeling of connectedness and energy. That sustains me as well. I know I am no longer a victim. I have gone from victim, to survivor to one who thrives. I believe in my inner voice (sometimes) and even listen to it (sometimes).

I love photography. When I was a small child, light and shadow fascinated me. I wanted the pictures I took to look as I imagined them in my head. Yet I never got a good camera until three years ago. Now I love taking pictures and creating my vision. I love looking at a scene and imagining how it would look in a photo and making that happen.

I never imagined my life turning out like this. I never imagined I would be a lawyer, a teacher, photographer, mother, and wife. I have a great job at the Transition Year Program at Dalhousie and Dalhousie Law School. I am glad to be alive and passionate about my life. I am no longer a victim. I am surrounded by love. I know that love can change my life. And that continues to heal me.

In August, 2000, my life changed again, even though change is probably not a strong enough word. Josh died in a car accident. I did not think I could go on after his death. I am still in pain and grieving but his death has taught me how precious life is. I think I am holding on to everyone just a bit tighter. I sense my life is moving in a different direction now. I feel that since Josh died, I have taken an inner journey. I will be giving up the Chair position and paying more attention to my family. The change I sensed coming in June certainly has occurred and more importantly, we must live our dreams, now!

I am still grieving and still working hard. I have talked long enough and I have told you my story. Now it is your turn. In the sacred talking circle, the one with the talking stick speaks without interruption. I thank you for allowing me this space and I now pass the stick to you . . . so let the circle continue, share your story.